Fix It!
Grammar

The Nose Tree

TEACHER'S MANUAL BOOK 1

Pamela White

THIRD EDITION

Also by Pamela White

Fix It! Grammar: The Nose Tree Student Book 1
Fix It! Grammar: Robin Hood Teacher's Manual Book 2
Fix It! Grammar: Robin Hood Student Book 2
Fix It! Grammar: Frog Prince, or Just Deserts Teacher's Manual Book 3
Fix It! Grammar: Frog Prince, or Just Deserts Student Book 3
Fix It! Grammar: Little Mermaid Teacher's Manual Book 4
Fix It! Grammar: Little Mermaid Student Book 4
Fix It! Grammar: Chanticleer Teacher's Manual Book 5
Fix It! Grammar: Chanticleer Student Book 5
Fix It! Grammar: Sir Gawain and the Green Knight Teacher's Manual Book 6
Fix It! Grammar: Sir Gawain and the Green Knight Student Book 6

The purchase of this book entitles its owner to a free download of *The Nose Tree* student Blackline Masters.

Go to: IEW.com/FIX-1-E

(See the blue page for complete download instructions.)

Institute for Excellence in Writing
8799 N. 387 Road
Locust Grove, OK 74352
800.856.5815
info@IEW.com
IEW.com

Printed in the United States of America

Accessing Your Downloads

The purchase of this book entitles its owner to a free download of the following:

- *Fix-It! Student Book 1* e-book (132 pages*)
- *Mastery Learning* e-audio
- *But, but, but ... What about Grammar?* e-audio

To download these e-resources, please follow the directions below:

1. Go to our website: IEW.com.

2. Log in to your online customer account. If you do not have an account, you will need to create one.

3. After you are logged in, go to this web page: IEW.com/FIX-1-E

4. Click the red arrow, and then click the checkboxes next to the names of the files you wish to place in your account.

5. Click the "Add to my files" button.

6. To access your files now and in the future, click on "Your Account" and click on the "Files" tab (one of the gray tabs).

7. Click on each file name to download the files onto your computer.

Please note: You are free to download and print the student e-book as needed for use within *your immediate family or classroom*. However, this information is proprietary, and we are trusting you to be on your honor not to share it with anyone. Please see the copyright page for further details. Thank you.

* If you would prefer to purchase *Fix It! Student Book 1* as a preprinted, spiral-bound book, it is available at this web page: IEW.com/FIX-1-SB.

If you have any difficulty receiving these downloads after going through the steps above, please call 800.856.5815.

Institute for Excellence in Writing
8799 N. 387 Road
Locust Grove, OK 74352

Welcome to *Fix It!*

Welcome to the first book of *Fix It! Grammar: The Nose Tree*. As your students enjoy reading a sentence or two of this fairy tale each day, they will learn to apply grammar rules to the writing. Over the course of the year, they will become experts in the basic parts of speech and some of the rules involved in writing.

This is not a traditional grammar program, so it will not feel as if you are really learning grammar. Instead, you and your students will be internalizing the tools necessary for editing their own compositions, which is the main goal of grammar.

The Method: Modeling Proper Grammar within Stories

The traditional method of teaching grammar is to present a grammar rule and then have students apply it in a series of contrived exercises. When that grammar rule is learned, another is taught and practiced in the same manner.

Although students often do well on these traditional worksheets, the learning does not usually transfer to their own writing and editing. Why? The grammar involved in real-life sentences is usually much more complicated than what is in the grammar exercise book, so students are often unable to edit their own work.

Fix It! Grammar overcomes these difficulties by teaching grammar at the point of need. Instead of a page full of grammar exercises, students will tackle real-life sentences with limited instruction. Thus, students will learn to think about their writing and incrementally learn how to apply the grammar rules to written work. Moreover, it is this daily practice in editing that will help instill the habit of editing anything they write.

For this to work, you as the teacher need to approach this book as a series of modeling exercises. Discuss each rule as it is presented, and then model for your students how to label the sentences and make the corrections. As your students gain confidence, they will often complete the labels and corrections accurately, but that is not always the case. Consider that mistakes are an opportunity to learn. If your students mismark a word or miss a correction, laugh! Show them what they missed, revisit the grammar rule involved, and encourage them that they can catch it next time.

After all, everyone needs an editor. Even professional writers and editors miss errors. The important thing is to understand the process and catch as much as you can. Knowing the reasons behind the fixes will make your students much better editors in the long run, and you will also gain the expertise to evaluate your students' papers better when they are older.

The Process: 15 Minutes a Day

This book is intended to provide 33 weeks of grammar instruction and practice. The process should take about fifteen minutes a day, four days a week. If you are using it with an older student, the book might be completed in a semester by doubling up the weeks.

If you are using this course with a writing class that meets weekly, we recommend having each family purchase the Teacher's Manual. Ask the parents to go over the passages at home with their children. That frees you up to focus on just some of the concepts so it does not take up too much class time.

Get Ready

Follow the instructions on the blue page in the front of this manual to download the student book. Print out one copy per student. You can also purchase a spiral-bound version of the student book at IEW.com/FIX-1-SB.

Student Notebook. If you printed a copy of the student book, each student will need a two-pocket notebook with three-hole fasteners to store the *Fix It* student pages. The lessons and student pages can be added to the middle section while the pockets may be used to house the Grammar Glossary, which students will not usually need at this level, and the Grammar Cards. If you purchased the spiral-bound student book, then all you need is a place to store the grammar cards.

Grammar Cards. At the back of the student book is a collection of grammar cards, which provide students with easy access to grammar terms and rules after the concepts are introduced in *Fix It* instructions. Students may keep the cards in a resealable plastic pouch or tape the cards to a piece of card stock so that they can easily flip the cards to see the back, as illustrated at right.

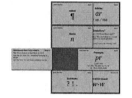

Spiral Notebook. Each day your student will be invited to record the vocabulary word with its definition and rewrite the passage neatly. The story rewrite can be kept in the front of a single-subject spiral notebook while the vocabulary list can be kept in the back.

Get Started

Begin the program by reading the directions presented on page 3 of the student book (page 7 of this Teacher's Manual). Tell your student that this program works like a puzzle. It is a series of daily games to practice the elements of grammar that they will learn over many weeks.

Your students will likely miss many of the fixes and markings as they work through the program, so stress that "a mistake is an opportunity to learn." They can use their mistakes to learn grammar better. Thus, keep the lessons light and fun, and teach your students to laugh and learn from the elements they miss.

Learn It

Start the week by reading through the "Learn It" section of the student book. Cut out the related grammar cards located near the back of the student book. Your student may keep these cards handy throughout the year and reference them as needed.

Next, show your student how to apply the lesson to the Day 1 passage. Model how to make the editing marks and grammar notations. Since all the markings are illustrated in this Teacher's Manual, you can easily guide your student.

The explanations below the edited text are for the teacher. The discussion notes provide you with the reasons behind each of the fixes as well as some of the other elements of grammar that may come up in your discussion.

Notice that they are organized into two sections: Fixes and Grammar Notations. You will likely need to reference the grammar notations in order to make the corrections, so do not feel that you have to follow the discussion notes in order. Simply use them as a reference as you work through the passage.

The Layout

You can teach the information in any order that makes sense to you and your students. To keep things organized, the material is arranged like this:

Fixes. These notes provide the reasons for each of the corrections. Use them to explain why a fix was needed or to quiz your students on their understanding.

Grammar Notations. These notes explain the grammar markings and suggest questions that can help you guide your student to see how the grammar works.

Do not feel like you need to read everything in these sections to your students. Teach at the point of need. If it is too much, teach less. If they know it already, skip it.

Style. This section is introduced in Week 9. The style section deals with dress-ups and typically appears on Day 4 of every week.

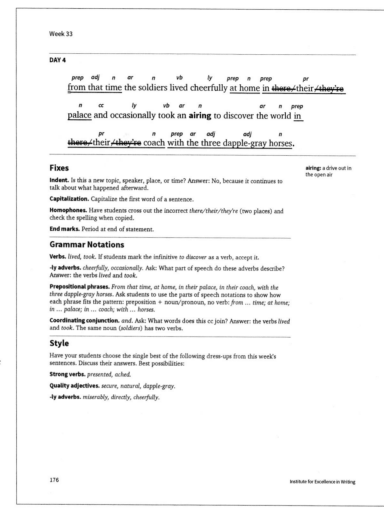

Sentences. At the beginning of each lesson is the student sentence with corrections.

Vocabulary words. These and their definitions are printed in the sidebar, along with other supporting notes.

Fix It

On the remaining three days of the week, continue to fix and mark the passage. Review the directions presented on page 7 of this Teacher's Manual and continue to model the process as needed. Students may do some of the lesson on their own, such as looking up the vocabulary word and attempting to fix and mark the passage. However, it can also be done together.

The discussion should not take more than fifteen minutes per day. If you cannot touch on everything in that period of time, that is fine.

Use the discussion notes as needed to explain the fixes and discuss the grammar involved. Use the questions to help your student understand the grammar better, but do not feel compelled to read it all to your student. The principles will be repeated over and over, so there is plenty of time to learn. The daily discussion and practice will bring mastery, so keep this part of the lesson light and fun.

In addition to the regular discussion of grammar, the discussion notes include advanced concepts, teacher's notes, and tidbits for the grammar lovers among you. These additions, set off with icons, are primarily for the teacher's information to explain something that might be confusing in the discussion. If a student is curious, go ahead and discuss those concepts. However, they are generally above the scope of this course and can be just for a teacher's enjoyment and training.

Rewrite

Finally, the rewrite is the key to success. By rewriting the passage and paying careful attention to detail, your student will internalize the corrections. For your convenience, the corrected passage rewrite is printed in the Teacher's Manual at the end of each week's fixes.

Pacing

Adjust the pace of the teaching as needed. If your student is not understanding all the details, then do not require him to add new markings until the previous ones are easy. This mastery learning approach should be fun and low stress. If your students start to groan when you say, "Time for *Fix It!*" something is wrong.

For more on a mastery learning approach to teaching, listen to Andrew Pudewa's "Mastery Learning" talk. It has been included as a free download with your *Fix It!* purchase. See the blue page in the front of this manual for download instructions.

Grammar Glossary

The Grammar Glossary, found at the end of the teacher and student books, is a tool that can be used for all six *Fix It! Grammar* books. It summarizes most of the information that is taught in the books. Reference it if you want a little more information than was provided with the passage. It will also be a handy grammar guide for your student to use in the future.

Grading

This course is intended to be used as a teaching tool and thus should not be graded. If you must assign a grade, assess the students' rewrite of the passage. You can simply choose one of the passages from the week to evaluate. The passage can be worth ten points. Deduct one point for each error.

Find Help

The scope and sequence for this book is on pages 178–180.

If you would like to see a demonstration of how to do the *Fix It!* lessons, please watch the webinar on the IEW website. It is on the *Fix It!* Overview page. See IEW.com/Fix.

The Institute for Excellence in Writing also provides teacher forums for those using our materials. It is a great place to meet other IEW teachers and find answers to specific writing and grammar questions. To join: IEW.com/forum

Instructions

Welcome to *Fix It! Grammar*. This year you can enjoy learning grammar by seeing how it works in a real-life story.

GET READY

To organize your work, you will need a two-pocket notebook with three-hole fasteners and a single-subject spiral notebook. If you have the spiral-bound *Fix It!* student book, then all you need is a single subject spiral notebook.

Use the center of the two-pocket notebook to collect the lesson and *Fix It!* pages as your teacher distributes them each week. Rewrite the passage in the front of the spiral notebook and use the back of the book to write down the vocabulary words and their definitions, working from the back forward.

Grammar cards are located in the back of the student book after page 72 and before the Grammar Glossary section. These may be cut out as they are needed and stored in a resealable plastic pouch or taped to a piece of card stock, as illustrated at right. The cards may be kept in the notebook pocket or tucked into the spiral-bound student book.

LEARN IT

With your teacher, read through the "Learn It" section for the week. This will show you what you will be looking for that week and for weeks to come.

To help you remember and review what you learned, use the grammar card(s) for the week. Keep them handy each time you work on *Fix It!* so that the information is at your fingertips.

FIX IT

Every Day	Read the sentence. Look up the bolded word in a dictionary. Decide which definition best fits the meaning of the word in this sentence. In the vocabulary section of your notebook, write a brief definition (using key words) labeled with the appropriate week. Add to this list every day.
Day 1	Read the instructions for the week with your teacher. Mark and fix the first passage with your teacher's help. Discuss what you missed with your teacher, and then complete the rewrite after fixing.
Days 2–4	Use the abbreviations at the top of the page along with the grammar cards to help you remember how to mark the passage. Your teacher will help you with anything you miss. Remember, a mistake is an opportunity to learn.
Rewrite	After marking, correcting, and discussing the passage with your teacher each day, copy the corrected passage into your notebook so that you end up with a handwritten copy of the complete story. Your teacher can show you an example of the rewrite in the teacher's book.

- Be sure to double-space.
- Do not copy the markings, just the story.
- Be careful to indent where indicated and use capital letters properly.
- Carefully copy the punctuation and use end marks.

Page 3, *Fix It! Grammar:* The Nose Tree, Student Book 1

Read this introductory page with your students.

Help your students set up their Fix It notebook as described in the Get Ready section.

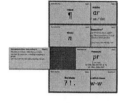

Notice that the first day of each week is a teaching day. Read through the Learn It part with your students and then show them exactly what to do using the Day 1 passage.

On the remaining days your students can complete the fixes independently before you go over them to ensure understanding.

Students will not be assigned reading in the Grammar Glossary, which is a tool you may use to learn more about a concept. The same glossary is in all six books, so it contains advanced information as well as basic.

Week 1

Nouns, Homophones, and End Marks

LEARN IT

Since this is the first day, there are several things you need to know to get started. But do not worry; they are easy! Read through these few things with your teacher, who will use the Day 1 passage to show you how they work.

Indent
Notice the ¶ symbol at the beginning of the Day 1 sentence. This is a paragraph mark, and it means that this sentence needs to start a new paragraph with an indent. In a later lesson you will learn the rules for when to begin a new paragraph.

For now, all you have to do is watch for the paragraph marks (¶). Whenever you see one at the start of a sentence, be sure to start a new paragraph when you copy the sentence into your notebook. Do not copy the ¶ symbol in your rewrite.

Nouns (*n*)
Grammarians have sorted words into different categories, and you can learn how to do it, too. They call these labels "parts of speech." This week you will look for nouns. Label them by printing a little *n* over each one.

Nouns are things, people, animals, places, and ideas. To determine if a word is a noun, apply these two tests, which work best for objects and animals:

1. Is it countable? *two* _____

2. Can an article come in front of it? *the* _____; *a/an* _____.

Homophones
Homophones are words that sound alike but are spelled differently and have different meanings. Where indicated with underlining, choose the correct homophone for *there*, *their*, or *they're* by crossing out the incorrect words. Use *there* when it is indicating a place (here or there), *their* when it belongs to someone, and *they're* when it is a contraction meaning *they are*.

End marks
You have likely learned that every sentence must have an end mark. End marks are missing in this week's sentences. Decide which kind of end mark (period, question mark, or exclamation point) each sentence needs and add it on.

To help you remember these things for future lessons, cut out the Week 1 grammar cards located in the back of this book. Keep them handy so you can reference them as needed.

FIX IT

Follow the process detailed on the previous page to complete the fixes this week.

- Read the sentence.
- Define the bolded vocabulary word.
- Fix and mark the sentence.
- Discuss your work with your teacher.
- Rewrite the sentence in another notebook.

Page 4, *Fix It! Grammar: Grammar* The Nose Tree, Student Book 1

Read the Learn It part with your students.

Because this is the first week, there are many things to cover. If it is too much, just choose one thing today and teach a new thing each day this week.

You have complete control over what you cover at what pace, so feel free to shorten lessons as needed.

Grammar Cards. Find the grammar cards in the back of the student book and cut out the ones that were covered in today's lesson. Have your students keep the cards handy so they can spread the cards out each day and use them for reference.

Once you have read the Learn It part, show your student how to apply it to the Day 1 passage.

✎ **Teacher's note.** As you progress through these lessons, you will find many things to address in each passage. You do not need to cover them all! Keep it light and make it a game. Your student does not have to master the elements the first time out. Over time with repetition, mastery will come.

Institute for Excellence in Writing

DAY 1

¶ Did you ever hear the story of the three **poor** soldiers?

(marked with n above "story" and n above "soldiers")

Show your student how to complete the Fix It part of the instructions. Cut out the Week 1 grammar cards located in the back of the student book. These cards can serve as reminders throughout the year.

Read the sentence. Read the sentence together. Explain to your student that you will be working on a story this year, one sentence per day.

Define the bolded vocabulary word. Find the bolded vocabulary word and talk about its meaning. If your students do not know the word, show them how to look it up in the dictionary. Choose the specific meaning that applies in this context.

Fix and mark the sentence. Mark the sentence as illustrated above.

Fixes

Indent. This sentence will start on a new line and include an indent of about ½ inch because it is the start of the story and therefore a new topic.

To help your students remember to indent when copying the passage into their notebook, the editing mark for *paragraph* (¶) has been added to the indented sentences on the student pages.

End marks. The sentence asks a question so closes with a question mark.

Once the passage is marked and you have discussed the marking with your students, show them how to begin their rewrite on a fresh sheet of paper. Review the rewrite instructions on page 3 of the Student Book (page 7 of this Teacher's Manual). Show your students what is meant by writing something double-spaced (by skipping a line between lines). Instruct them to indent when indicated and include capital letters and punctuation. They should not copy the markings.

Grammar Notations

Nouns to mark with *n*: *story, soldiers.*

Guide students to find nouns they missed with hints and questions. E.g., "I found two nouns in this passage, one referring to some people and the other a thing. Can you find either? Hint: the word *the* always has a noun close after it."

Rewrite. Each day, after students mark, correct, and discuss the passage with you, they should copy the corrected passage into a separate notebook so that, by the end of the class, they have a handwritten copy of the complete story. You can show them the examples of rewrites from this teacher's book.

Students should follow these guidelines:
- Be sure to double-space.
- Do not copy the markings, just the story.
- Be careful to indent where indicated and use capital letters properly.
- Carefully copy the punctuation and use end marks.

poor: lacking sufficient money. Explain that many words have more than one meaning, but the student's job is to write the meaning that *best* fits the context. In this case, *poor* could also mean unhappy or unfortunate, but *destitute* in the second sentence suggests that *impoverished* is the best meaning.

🖊 **Teacher's note.** The rules for indentation will be taught Week 12. If you wish to read them now for your reference, see Grammar Glossary: Additional Rules and Concepts: Indentation Rules, page G-29.

🖊 **Teacher's note.** The paragraph mark is called a "pilcrow," and it was created in the Middle Ages to separate content and predates actual paragraphs.

DAY 2

n n

They had fought well in the wars, but now they were out of work and

destitute.

Invite your students to mark the sentence as described on Day 1. When they are done, use the passage to discuss the markings. When the discussion is complete, students may begin their rewrite. Continue this process as you work through the book.

destitute: without enough money for basic survival; impoverished

Fixes

End mark. This is a statement so add a period.

Grammar Notations

Nouns to mark with *n*: *wars, work*. Remind your students that nouns always follow close after the word *the*.

Advanced. If students recognize that *they* is a noun, praise them for it! It is actually a pronoun, but most pronouns are basically types of nouns. However, this is an advanced concept that will be addressed later.

Advanced concepts are included here for your reference, but you do not need to discuss them with your students.

DAY 3

          n   n   n

They had journeyed a long way, sick at heart with their wretched luck.

Fixes

Homophones. Review *there/their/they're* because it will show up in the next passage.

- *there* = the adverb pointing to a place or point

- *their* = the possessive pronoun

- *they're* = the contraction for *they are*, which does not appear anywhere in the story since it is told in past tense

  Discuss the spelling of each word, especially *their*.

End marks. This is a statement so add a period.

wretched: very unfortunate in condition or circumstances

Grammar Notations

Nouns to mark with *n*: *way, heart, luck*. Praise students if they count *they* as a noun.

  Tests to determine if a word is a noun:

- If it is a person or thing, it is a noun.

- If it has *a*, *an*, or *the* in front of it, it is a noun. Sometimes there are adjectives in between, as in "a long way." Also, if it is a word that could have *a*, *an*, or *the* in front of it, it is likely a noun: "with *the luck* they had."

- If it is something you can count (such as *two ways* or *two hearts*), it is likely a noun.

DAY 4

¶ One evening ~~there~~/their ~~/they're~~ road brought them to a deep,

n (above *there/their*) ... *n* (above *they're*)

gloomy wood.

n (above *gloomy*)

Fixes

Indent. Start a new paragraph because of a switch in time. To begin a new paragraph, write on a new line and indent ½ inch.

Homophone. Have students cross out the incorrect *there/their/they're* and write the correct one in their rewrite.

> Remind them to check the spelling of *their* since it does not fit the usual "*i* before *e*" spelling rule (*i* before *e*, except after *c* or when sounding like *a* as in *neighbor* or *weigh*).

End marks. Period at end of statement.

Grammar Notations

Nouns to mark with *n*: *evening, road, wood.*

> Apply the noun tests (see Week 1 Day 3 and Grammar Glossary: Parts of Speech: Nouns, page G-5). All three could have more than one (*two evenings, two roads, two woods*), so they are nouns. *Wood* also has the article *a* (plus two adjectives) before it, which signals a noun to follow.

> Students may have trouble recognizing that *evening* is a thing since we do not touch it as we could a *road* or *wood*. Ask them: Can you put *a, an,* or *the* in front of it? Could we say "an evening" or "the evening" here instead of "one evening"? Could we have two evenings? Yes to all these questions, so it is a noun.

---

gloomy: deeply shaded; dark; dismal

✏ **Teacher's note.** The thin underline in the student book, such as under *there/their/they're*, indicates a place in the text for the student to do an additional task, such as choose the correct word or, in later lessons, make a contraction or create a possessive.

✏ **Teacher's note.** Have the students refer to the Week 1 grammar cards from the back of the student book.

STUDENT REWRITE

Did you ever hear the story of the three poor soldiers? They had fought well in the wars, but now they were out of work and destitute. They had journeyed a long way, sick at heart with their wretched luck.

One evening their road brought them to a deep, gloomy wood.

Week 2

Articles

LEARN IT

Articles (ar)   Now that you can identify nouns, it is time find another part of speech: the article. Articles are easy because there are only three of them.

a, an, the

Articles always set up a noun. When you see an article, a noun is sure to follow, although sometimes a describing word may come in between, as in "a small dwarf." Label articles by printing a little *ar* over each one.

To help you remember these things for future lessons, add the Week 2 grammar card to your collection. Keep the Week 1 cards handy for review.

FIX IT

Read   Read the sentence.

Vocabulary   Look up the bolded word in a dictionary and decide which definition best fits the meaning of the word in this sentence. Add the definition to the list in the back of your notebook.

Day 1   Your teacher will help you mark and fix the first passage. Complete the rewrite after fixing.

Days 2–4   Use the abbreviations at the top of the next page and the grammar cards to help you remember how to mark the passage. Your teacher will help you with anything you miss. Remember, a mistake is an opportunity to learn.

Rewrite   After marking, correcting, and discussing the passage with your teacher each day, copy the corrected passage into a separate notebook so that you end up with a handwritten copy of the complete story.

- Be sure to double-space.
- Do not copy the markings, just the story.
- Be careful to indent where indicated and use capital letters properly.
- Carefully copy the punctuation and use end marks.

Read the Learn It part with your students.

If your student is not ready for new information, consider teaching it in a later week. You have complete control over what you cover at what pace, so feel free to adjust the lessons as needed.

Grammar Cards. Have your students find the new grammar card to add to their collection. Remind them to use the cards as needed to mark the passages.

Once you have read the Learn It part, show your student how to apply it to the Day 1 passage.

✏ **Teacher's note.** Remember, keep the discussions light. If your students begin to groan when you say "Time for *Fix It!*" something is wrong. Make it more like a game than a lesson.

DAY 1

       ar   *n*

Since the wood was dark and dangerous, they decided to take turns **keeping**

watch.

Fixes

End marks. Period at end of statement.

keeping watch:
acting as a guard;
watching with great
attention

Grammar Notations

Articles to mark with *ar*: *the*. Reminder: articles must be followed by a noun, even if there are adjectives in between: *the wood, a long way*.

Nouns to mark with *n*: *wood*.

Praise students if they mark *they* as a noun since it functions just like one.

✧ **Advanced.** *turns* and *watch* are also nouns but easily confused with other parts of speech. Do not worry about teaching words or concepts labeled *advanced* but praise students if they mark them.

DAY 2

   n   *ar n*   *ar n*   *ar n*

Two of them fell asleep under a tree while the third built a fire and stayed

alert.

Fixes

End marks. Period at end of statement.

alert: fully aware and
wide awake

Grammar Notations

Nouns. *Two, tree, third, fire.* Have students identify which nouns have articles: *a tree, the third, a fire.*

✧ **Advanced.** The nouns *two* and *third* are advanced. Numbers sometimes function as nouns, as do *two* and *third* here, instead of as adjectives. You can tell they are adjectives, not nouns, if they describe a noun, as in "two soldiers," which these do not.

Articles marked with *ar*: *a, the, a.*

DAY 3

ar   *n*

¶ He had not sat long before, all of a sudden, up came a small **dwarf** in

ar   *n*

a red jacket.

Fixes

dwarf: in folklore, a very short man with magical powers

Indent. Start a new paragraph because of a new topic, the appearance of the dwarf.

End marks. Period at end of statement.

Grammar Notations

Articles. *a, a.* Ask students to read the articles aloud with their nouns and without the adjectives that come between: *a dwarf, a jacket.*

> ✧ **Advanced.** *All of a sudden* is an idiom, which is an expression that cannot be understood literally, word for word. Do not worry about parts of speech in idioms. If your student marks them, that is also fine.

Nouns. *dwarf, jacket.*

DAY 4

ar   *n*   *ar*   *n*

Rather than **rebuffing** the little man, the soldier invited him to come warm

ar *n*

himself by the fire.

Fixes

rebuffing: driving away; rejecting

End marks. Period at end of statement.

Grammar Notations

Articles. *the, the, the.*

Nouns. *man, soldier, fire.*

> Ask students to read the articles aloud with their nouns: *the man, the soldier, the fire.*

STUDENT REWRITE

Since this passage continues without another indentation, be sure students continue writing where last week's passage left off.

Since the wood was dark and dangerous, they decided to take turns keeping watch. Two of them fell asleep under a tree while the third built a fire and stayed alert.

He had not sat long before, all of a sudden, up came a small dwarf in a red jacket. Rather than rebuffing the little man, the soldier invited him to come warm himself by the fire.

Week 3

Quotations

LEARN IT

Quotations   When someone speaks in a story, we use quotation marks. The quotation marks are included in the fixes. Your job will be to copy the quotation marks (" ") carefully and the punctuation around them.

These are the quotation rules that are followed in these Fix Its:

- Enclose what someone says in quotation marks but not the narration that sets up a quotation.
- When the speaker continues with more than one sentence, do not add closing quotation marks (") until the end of his speech. Sometimes a speech will cover more than one day's assignment.
- Commas and periods go inside closing quotation marks.
- If narration interrupts a speech, use commas on both sides of the interruption. Commas "hug" the word they follow—that is, they come right next to it—not the word after them.

To help you remember these things for future lessons, add the Week 3 grammar card to your collection. Keep the remaining cards handy for review.

FIX IT

Read   Read the sentence.

Vocabulary   Look up the bolded word in a dictionary and decide which definition best fits the meaning of the word in this sentence. Add the definition to the list in the back of your notebook.

Day 1   Your teacher will help you mark and fix the first passage. Complete the rewrite after fixing.

Days 2–4   Use the abbreviations at the top of the next page and the grammar cards to help you remember how to mark the passage. Your teacher will help you with anything you miss. Remember, a mistake is an opportunity to learn.

Rewrite   Copy the corrected passage into a separate notebook.

- Be sure to double-space.
- Do not copy the markings, just the story.
- Be careful to indent where indicated and use capital letters properly.
- Carefully copy the punctuation and use end marks.

Page 8, *Fix It! Grammar:* **The Nose Tree, Student Book 1**

If your student is not ready for new information, consider teaching it in a later week. You have complete control over what you cover at what pace, so feel free to adjust the lessons as needed.

Grammar Cards. Have your students find the new grammar card to add to their collection. Remind them to use the cards as needed to mark the passages.

✏ **Teacher's note.** Note that true quotation marks are "curly," not straight. The straight marks are most commonly used as prime symbols for measurements, such as for feet and inches (6' 2") — note that true prime marks are slightly angled.

Why do straight marks exist? Because typewriters had only so many keys, combining all double quote marks and single quote marks (and apostrophes!) into two keys was essential.

DAY 1

As they talked, he told the little man about ~~there~~/*their* ~~they're~~ **plight.**
(above: ar, n, n)

Fixes

plight: an unfortunate condition or situation

Homophones. Have students cross out the incorrect *there/their/they're*. Remind them to check the spelling of *their* when they copy it into their notebook.

End marks. Period at end of statement.

Grammar Notations

Articles and nouns. Mark as illustrated. Articles: *the*. Continue to apply the noun tests illustrated on the grammar cards as needed: *the man; the plight or two plights*.

✧ **Advanced.** Praise students if they also mark *they* or *he* as nouns. These are pronouns but function just like nouns here.

✎ **Teacher's note.** Not every grammar notation will be included in the discussion notes. Continue to discuss the parts of speech as needed.

DAY 2

¶ "Well, my **worthy** fellow," stated the little man, "I will do what I can

for you.
(above: n, ar, n)

Fixes

worthy: having great merit and good character

Indent. Start a new paragraph because there is a new speaker.

Quotations. Use quotation marks to enclose all his words. Do not close with quotation marks, however, because he is not finished speaking. Tomorrow's lesson continues his speech.

Commas. For teacher information: The narration ("stated the little man") interrupts his spoken words so needs the commas on both sides of it. Your students do not need to know this yet, but be sure to check that they copy the comma after *fellow* inside the closing quotes and include the comma after *man*.

✎ **Teacher's note.** Read about quotations in the punctuation section of the Grammar Glossary (page G-19).

End marks. Period at end of statement, but no close quotes because he is not finished speaking. Continue writing next time where you left off.

Grammar Notations

Articles and nouns. Mark as indicated.

DAY 3

n   *n*   *ar*   *n*
Take this cloak and show it to your **comrades** in the morning.

Fixes

Quotations. Explain that the little man is still speaking but there are no quotation marks since it is in the middle of a continued speech.

End marks. Period at end of statement. but no close quotes because he is not finished speaking.

comrades: close friends; companions; people who share in each other's activities

Grammar Notations

Articles and nouns. Mark as indicated.

> If students have trouble seeing that *morning* (which we cannot touch) is a noun, apply the two noun tests: "the morning" or "two mornings."

DAY 4

ar   *n*
Whenever you **don** the cloak, anything you wish for will be done for you."

Fixes

Quotations. No open quotation marks since this continues his speech from Week 3 Day 3, but because he finishes speaking here, the sentence closes with quotation marks.

End marks. Period at end of statement. He is finished speaking, so it closes with quotations. Check that your student puts the period inside the closing quotations.

don: put on; dress in

Grammar Notations

Articles and nouns. Mark as indicated.

> ✧ **Advanced.** If students identify *anything* as a noun, praise them. It is actually a pronoun. If they do not identify it at all, that is fine.

STUDENT REWRITE

Since this passage continues without another indentation, be sure students continue writing where last week's passage left off.

As they talked, he told the little man about their plight.

"Well, my worthy fellow," stated the little man, "I will do what I can for you. Take this cloak and show it to your comrades in the morning. Whenever you don the cloak, anything you wish for will be done for you."

Week 4

Pronouns

LEARN IT

Pronouns (*pr*)   In Week 1 you learned about nouns (people, places, and things).

Personal pronouns are like nouns. They refer back to some person or thing recently mentioned and substitute for that person or thing. In the sentence, "Take this *cloak* and show *it* to your comrades in the morning," the personal pronoun *it* refers to the cloak mentioned earlier in the sentence.

Label pronouns by printing *pr* above the personal pronouns in the passages. Here is a list of pronouns to look for:

I, me, you
he, him, his, she, her, it, its
we, they, them, their

To help you remember these things for future lessons, add the Week 4 grammar card to your collection. Keep the remaining cards handy for review.

FIX IT

Read	Read the sentence.
Vocabulary	Look up the bolded word in a dictionary and decide which definition best fits the meaning of the word in this sentence. Add the definition to the list in the back of your notebook.
Day 1	Your teacher will help you mark and fix the first passage. Complete the rewrite after fixing.
Days 2–4	Use the abbreviations at the top of the next page and the grammar cards to help you remember how to mark the passage. Your teacher will help you with anything you miss. Remember, a mistake is an opportunity to learn.
Rewrite	Copy the corrected passage into a separate notebook.

- Be sure to double-space.
- Do not copy the markings, just the story.
- Be careful to indent where indicated and use capital letters properly.
- Carefully copy the punctuation and use end marks.

Page 10, *Fix It! Grammar:* **The Nose Tree, Student Book 1**

Read the Learn It part with your students.

Adjust the lessons as needed.

Grammar Cards. Have your students find the new grammar card to add to their collection. The pronoun grammar card has a list of pronouns for your student to look for.

Pronouns. To keep it simple, the list includes all subjective and objective pronouns that appear in *Nose Tree* as well as the four possessive pronouns that appear frequently.

Infrequently used possessive and reflexive pronouns are not in the list but will be mentioned in notes when they appear. Students do not need to label *who, whom,* or *whose* as pronouns. For a chart of all these pronouns, see *Grammar Glossary* page G-7.

DAY 1

ar   *n*

The **elfin** man bowed and walked away.

Fixes

End marks. Period at end of statement.

elfin: like an elf, small and merry or mischievous

Grammar Notations

Articles and nouns. Mark as illustrated. Use the noun tests as needed.

DAY 2

n   *ar*   *n*

¶ **In due time** the second soldier's turn to watch came.

Fixes

Indent. Start a new paragraph because of a new topic, the second soldier.

End marks. Period at end of statement.

in due time: at the appropriate time

Grammar Notations

Articles and nouns. Mark as illustrated.

✧ **Advanced.** Some students may think of *turn* as a verb. Remind them that some words can function as more than one part of speech; no one is turning, so it is not used as a verb but a noun here.

✧ **Advanced.** *Soldier's* is a possessive noun, but marking them at this level is not required. Possessive nouns are nouns that function as adjectives. Some grammar programs call them adjectives; some call them nouns. Fortunately, it does not really matter because it will not affect punctuation or grammar so long as students recognize that possessive nouns need an apostrophe.

DAY 3

pr   *ar*   *n*   *ar*   *n*
He **likewise** was visited by the little man in the red jacket.

Fixes

End marks. Period at end of statement.

likewise: in the same way; in like manner

Grammar Notations

Articles, nouns, and pronouns. Mark as indicated above. Discuss as needed.

DAY 4

ar   *n*   *pr*   *ar*   *n*   *pr*   *n*
The soldier treated him in as **sociable** a way as his comrade had done.

Fixes

End marks. Period at end of statement.

sociable: friendly; agreeable

Grammar Notations

Articles and nouns. Help your students use the noun test: *The soldier; a way. Comrade* could have *the* in front of it or be countable (*two comrades*), so it also passes the noun tests.

Pronouns. *him, his.*

♡ **Grammar lovers.** *Him* is an objective pronoun since it functions as the direct object of the verb *treated. His comrade* means the comrade belonging to him, so *his* is possessive.

STUDENT REWRITE

Since this passage continues without another indentation, be sure students continue writing where last week's passage left off.

The elfin man bowed and walked away.

In due time the second soldier's turn to watch came. He likewise was visited by the little man in the red jacket. The soldier treated him in as sociable a way as his comrade had done.

Week 5

Read the Learn It part with your students.

Adjust the lessons as needed.

Which Clauses

LEARN IT

Which clause (w-w)
If you have been doing Excellence in Writing, you have likely heard of dress-ups. These are stylistic techniques used to dress-up our writing.

One of the dress-ups is a *who-which* (w-w) clause. This week, look for *which* clauses.

Label the *which* by printing a little *w-w* over each one.

The clause will include more words than just a *which*, so read the entire clause from the *which* to the next comma or end mark.

To help you remember these things for future lessons, add the grammar card for Weeks 5 and 6 to your collection. Keep the remaining cards handy for review.

The **who-which clause** is a dress-up in IEW's Structure and Style writing program. If you are not doing Structure and Style, simply introduce this as a part of grammar. For more information, see the Grammar Glossary: Stylistic Techniques, page G-35. This week the *which* clause will be identified.

Grammar Cards. Have your students find the new grammar card to add to their collection.

Once you have read the Learn It part, show your student how to apply it to the Day 1 passage.

FIX IT

Read
Read the sentence.

Vocabulary
Look up the bolded word in a dictionary and decide which definition best fits the meaning of the word in this sentence. Add the definition to the list in the back of your notebook.

Day 1
Your teacher will help you mark and fix the first passage. Complete the rewrite after fixing.

Days 2–4
Use the abbreviations at the top of the next page and the grammar cards to help you remember how to mark the passage. Your teacher will help you with anything you miss. Remember, a mistake is an opportunity to learn.

Rewrite
Copy the corrected passage into a separate notebook.

- Be sure to double-space.
- Do not copy the markings, just the story.
- Be careful to indent where indicated and use capital letters properly.
- Carefully copy the punctuation and use end marks.

Page 12, *Fix It! Grammar:* **The Nose Tree, Student Book 1**

DAY 1

       ar   *n*   *ar*   *n* *ar* *n*   *w-w*

The little man gave the second soldier a **purse**, which would always be full of

       n   *pr*   *pr*

gold, he told him.

Fixes

End marks. Period at end of statement.

Grammar Notations

Articles and nouns. *The man, the soldier, a purse.* Can you say "the gold"? Yes, so *gold* is also a noun.

Which clauses. Have students locate and read the entire *who-which* clause to you: *which would always be full of gold.* Show them that *which* describes the noun (*purse*) that comes immediately before it.

> **purse:** a small pouch for carrying money
>
> Note the context: this is not a typical woman's purse but a small bag, which men used to carry instead of wallets.

DAY 2

                  ar   *n*   *w-w*   *ar*

After **awarding** the gift, which truthfully reflected the soldier's generous

      n   *ar*   *n*

heart, the little man again bowed and walked away.

Fixes

End marks. Period at end of statement.

> **awarding:** giving something as earned or merited

Grammar Notations

Articles and nouns. *the gift, the heart, the man.*

  ✧ **Advanced.** No need to discuss *soldier's* as a possessive noun.

Which clauses. Mark with *w-w* and read aloud: *which truthfully reflected the soldier's generous heart.* Point out that *which* describes the noun (*gift*) that comes immediately before it.

DAY 3

>   *ar*   *n*   *n*   *pr*   *ar*
> ¶ When the third soldier's turn to watch came, he also had the little
>
> *n*   *ar*   *n*   *pr*   *n*   *pr*
> man in the red jacket for his guest and also treated him **graciously.**

Fixes

Indent. Start a new paragraph because of a new topic, what happened to the third soldier.

End marks. Period at end of statement.

> **graciously:** in a kind and courteous manner

Grammar Notations

Articles and nouns. Ask your student to read the nouns that go with each article: *the soldier's turn, the man, the jacket.*

DAY 4

>   *ar*   *n*   *pr ar*   *n*   *w-w*   *n*   *n*
> The little man gave him a **curious** horn, which would bring help in time of
>
>   *n*   *pr*
> need when it was blown.

Fixes

End marks. Period at end of statement.

> **curious:** odd; strange; arousing interest

Grammar Notations

Articles and nouns. *the man, a horn, help, time, need.*

- ✦ **Advanced.** Some students may have trouble recognizing that *help, time,* and *need* are all nouns, and this is OK! Either skip marking these or point out that all could have *the* in front of them: *the help, the time, the need.*

- ✎ **Teacher's note.** Some of the nouns do not lend themselves to the "two ____" test as easily as some others, but do not worry about teaching this. They are similar to abstract nouns like *love,* which are not countable.

> We usually use this word to mean "eager to know" or "inquisitive," but the horn itself is not eager to know anything; it rather stirs our curiosity.

Pronouns. Ask students: What noun does *it* refer back to? Answer: *horn.*

***Who-which* clauses.** Mark with *w-w* and read aloud: *which would bring help in time of need.* Ask students to identify the noun that *which* describes: *horn.* Show that it comes immediately before the *which* clause.

STUDENT REWRITE

Since this passage continues without another indentation, be sure students continue writing where last week's passage left off.

The little man gave the second soldier a purse, which would always be full of gold, he told him. After awarding the gift, which truthfully reflected the soldier's generous heart, the little man again bowed and walked away.

When the third soldier's turn to watch came, he also had the little man in the red jacket for his guest and also treated him graciously. The little man gave him a curious horn, which would bring help in time of need when it was blown.

Week 6

Who Clauses

LEARN IT

***Who* Clause (*w-w*)**	The *who-which* clause is a dress-up. Last week you looked for the *which* clauses. This week, you will find a *who* clause as well.
	Label the *who* or the *which* by printing a little *w-w* over each one.
	Read the entire clause from the *who* or *which* to the next comma or end mark.
	The interesting thing about a *who-which* clause is that it provides more information about someone or something. When you find one, decide what noun the *who* or *which* clause describes.

To help you remember these things for future lessons, refer to the grammar card for Weeks 5 and 6 in your collection. Keep the remaining cards handy for review.

FIX IT

Read	Read the sentence.
Vocabulary	Look up the bolded word in a dictionary and decide which definition best fits the meaning of the word in this sentence. Add the definition to the list in the back of your notebook.
Day 1	Your teacher will help you mark and fix the first passage. Complete the rewrite after fixing.
Days 2–4	Use the abbreviations at the top of the next page and the grammar cards to help you remember how to mark the passage. Your teacher will help you with anything you miss. Remember, a mistake is an opportunity to learn.
Rewrite	Copy the corrected passage into a separate notebook.

  - Be sure to double-space.
  - Do not copy the markings, just the story.
  - Be careful to indent where indicated and use capital letters properly.
  - Carefully copy the punctuation and use end marks.

Read the Learn It part with your students.

Adjust the lessons as needed.

This week the ***who* clause** will be identified.

Grammar Cards. Have your students find the new grammar card to add to their collection.

Once you have read the Learn It part, show your student how to apply it to the Day 1 passage.

◀ **Listen.** This program teaches grammar through mastery learning. To learn more about this process, see the blue page of this book for a free MP3 download entitled "Mastery Learning."

Page 14, *Fix It! Grammar:* The Nose Tree, Student Book 1

DAY 1

ar   *n*   *ar*   *n*   *w-w*   *ar*   *n*

¶ In the morning the soldiers, who were **dumbfounded** by the events of

ar   *n*   *pr*   *n*   *ar*   *n*

the night before, shared ~~there~~/their ~~/they're~~ stories of the little man.

Fixes

Indent. Start a new paragraph because of a new time.

Homophones. Tell students to cross out the incorrect *there/their/they're* and check the spelling when copied. *Their stories* means the stories belonging to them, so *their* is possessive.

End marks. Period at end of statement.

dumbfounded: made nearly speechless with amazement; astonished

Grammar Notations

Articles and nouns. All the nouns except *stories* are clearly nouns because they have an article (*the*) in front of them. *Stories* passes both noun tests because the sentence could have read "*the* stories" (article) or "their *three* stories" (countable).

Who-which clauses. Mark with *w-w* and read aloud: *who were dumbfounded by the events of the night before.* Ask: What noun does this *who* clause describe? Answer: *soldiers*. Where is the noun? Answer: immediately before the *who* clause.

> ✧ **Advanced.** Point out that *who-which* clauses are often set off with commas. They take two commas, one before the *who* or *which* and one after the clause, unless the sentence ends with the *who-which* clause.

✎ **Teacher's note.** In the remaining grammar notations, not all the parts of speech will be discussed. Continue to check them and discuss as needed.

DAY 2

pr   *n*   *pr*   *ar*   *n*

Since they were longtime friends, they agreed to use the purse and journey

ar   *n*

together to **survey** the world.

Fixes

End marks. Period at end of statement.

survey: to look at or take a general view of

Grammar Notations

Nouns. *friends, purse, world.*

> ✧ **Advanced.** Some students might mark *journey* as a noun. Sometimes it is, but here it is a verb form expressing an action. Again, though, it is not critical that students at this age understand all these concepts.

DAY 3

               n   *n*   *w-w*   *pr*   *pr*

¶ After several weeks of travel, which pleased them, they decided to

settle down.

Fixes

settle down: to stop moving around and live in a new country or place

Indent. Start a new paragraph because of a new time.

End marks. Period at end of statement.

Grammar Notations

Who-which **clauses.** Mark with *w-w* and read aloud: *which pleased them.*

Ask: What noun does this *which* clause describe? Answer: *travel.* Where is it? Answer: Right before the *which.*

Ask students to show you where the commas are placed (before the *which* and after the whole clause).

DAY 4

     ar   *n*   *pr*   *n*   *ar*   *n*

The first soldier put on his **wondrous** cloak and wished for a fine castle,

   w-w   *pr*   *n*

which would be ~~there/~~their~~/they're~~ home.

Fixes

wondrous: remarkable; exciting wonder

Homophones. Tell students to cross out the incorrect *there/their/they're* and check the spelling when copied.

End marks. Period at end of statement.

Grammar Notations

Teacher's note. Continue to apply the noun tests as needed (the _____, countable).

Who-which **clauses.** Mark with *w-w* and read aloud: *which would be their home.*

Ask: What noun immediately before it does this *which* clause describe? Answer: *castle.*

Ask students to show you where the commas are placed.

STUDENT REWRITE

In the morning the soldiers, who were dumbfounded by the events of the night before, shared their stories of the little man. Since they were longtime friends, they agreed to use the purse and journey together to survey the world.

After several weeks of travel, which pleased them, they decided to settle down. The first soldier put on his wondrous cloak and wished for a fine castle, which would be their home.

Week 7

Read the Learn It part with your students.

Adjust the lessons as needed.

This week action **verbs** will be identified.

Grammar Cards. Have your students find the new grammar card to add to their collection.

Once you have read the Learn It part, show your student how to apply it to the Day 1 passage.

Action Verbs

LEARN IT

Verb (*vb*)   Another part of speech is the verb. This week you will find action verbs.

Action verbs express action (as in *chop, budge, confide*) or ownership (as in *have, possess, own*).

Find the action verbs and label them by printing a little *vb* over each one.

To help you remember these things for future lessons, add the Week 7 grammar card to your collection. Keep the remaining cards handy for review.

FIX IT

Read   Read the sentence.

Vocabulary   Look up the bolded word in a dictionary and decide which definition best fits the meaning of the word in this sentence. Add the definition to the list in the back of your notebook.

Day 1   Your teacher will help you mark and fix the first passage. Complete the rewrite after fixing.

Days 2–4   Use the abbreviations at the top of the next page and the grammar cards to help you remember how to mark the passage. Your teacher will help you with anything you miss. Remember, a mistake is an opportunity to learn.

Rewrite   Copy the corrected passage into a separate notebook.

- Be sure to double-space.
- Do not copy the markings, just the story.
- Be careful to indent where indicated and use capital letters properly.
- Carefully copy the punctuation and use end marks.

Page 16, *Fix It! Grammar:* The Nose Tree, Student Book 1

DAY 1

   ar   n   pr vb   *pr*   *n*

In a **trice** it stood before ~~there~~/their~~/they're~~ eyes.

Fixes

trice: a very short time; an instant

Homophones. Tell students to cross out the incorrect *there/their/they're* and check the spelling when copied.

End marks. Period at end of statement.

Grammar Notations

Nouns. *trice, eyes.*

> ✧ **Advanced.** *Trice* probably will not sound like a noun, partly because it is not an object or person we can see. Discuss with students the noun tests: it has the article *a* in front of it, so it must be a noun.

Pronouns. Ask: What does *it* refer back to? Answer: *the castle.*

DAY 2

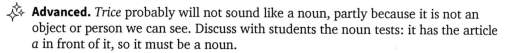

   n   *w-w*   *vb*   *n*   *n*   *w-w*   *vb*

Fine gardens, which displayed rare roses, and wide lawns, which contained

  ar   *n*   *vb*   *ar*   *n*

the softest grass, **encircled** the castle.

Fixes

encircled: surrounded; formed a circle around

End marks. Period at end of statement.

Grammar Notations

***Who-which* clauses.** There are two of them. Mark with *w-w* and read aloud: *which displayed rare roses; which contained the softest grass.*

> Ask: What nouns do these *which* clauses describe? Answer: *gardens, lawns.* This is advanced, so if your students do not see this on their own, simply tell them the answer.

> Ask students to show you where the commas are placed (before the *which*'s and after the clauses).

DAY 3

n   *n*   *n*   *n*   *n*   *vb*
Abundant flocks of sheep and plentiful herds of goats and oxen grazed about.

Fixes

End marks. Period at end of statement.

abundant: well supplied; more than enough

Grammar Notations

Verbs. *grazed.* Tell students that someone or something is always doing the verb action. Ask: Who is grazing? Answer: *flocks and herds* (a double subject) *grazed.*

If students say *sheep, goats,* and *oxen* are the subject, it is fine (see explanation below). If they do not see that there is more than one subject with the same verb, simply show it to them. Do not expect them to have mastered these concepts.

♡ **Grammar lovers.** *sheep, goats,* and *oxen* are actually the objects of the preposition *of,* not the true subjects of the verb *grazed.* However, this distinction is too advanced for most students of this age. (Prepositions will be introduced in Week 19.)

✎ **Teacher's note.** Read about noun functions in the Parts of Speech section of the Grammar Glossary (page G-6).

DAY 4

ar   n   vb ar   n   n   w-w

Out of the gate came a grand coach with three **dapple-gray** horses, which

vb   pr   pr   n

would bring them to ~~there~~/their ~~/they're~~ home.

Fixes

End marks. Period at end of statement.

Homophones. Tell students to cross out the incorrect *there/their/they're* and check the spelling when copied.

Grammar Notations

Verbs. *came, bring.*

⚙ **Advanced.** The subject of *came* is *coach*. Usually nouns come before verbs, but sometimes that order is reversed.

Who-which clauses. Mark with *w-w* and read aloud: *which would bring them to their home.* Ask: What noun immediately before *which* does this *which* clause describe? Answer: *horses.*

Ask students to show you where the commas are placed. Here, you need one before the *which* but none after the clause since this *which* clause comes at the end of the sentence.

♡ **Grammar lovers.** In *who-which* clauses, the subject is usually the *who* or *which.* In this clause, the verb is *would bring* and the subject *which.* You will introduce helping verbs like *would* in a later lesson.

> **dapple-gray:** gray with spots of darker shades. *Dapple* means clustered spots of a different color.

> ✏ **Teacher's note.** Students do not need to master subjects at this time. The discussion is intended to raise awareness.

STUDENT REWRITE

Since this passage continues without another indentation, be sure students continue writing where last week's passage left off.

In a trice it stood before their eyes. Fine gardens, which displayed rare roses, and wide lawns, which contained the softest grass, encircled the castle. Abundant flocks of sheep and plentiful herds of goats and oxen grazed about. Out of the gate came a grand coach with three dapple-gray horses, which would bring them to their home.

Week 8

Read the Learn It part with your students.

Adjust the lessons as needed.

This week students will identify **strong verbs**, which are another one of the Structure and Style dress-ups.

There are **no new grammar cards** for this lesson, but your students can continue to use the ones they have for review.

Once you have read the Learn It part, show your student how to apply it to the Day 1 passage.

Strong Verbs

LEARN IT

Verb (vb)   As you label the verbs, be on the lookout for especially strong verbs. Strong verbs give a strong image or feeling.

There are no new grammar cards for this lesson, but keep using your other cards for review.

FIX IT

Read   Read the sentence.

Vocabulary   Look up the bolded word in a dictionary and decide which definition best fits the meaning of the word in this sentence. Add the definition to the list in the back of your notebook.

Day 1   Your teacher will help you mark and fix the first passage. Complete the rewrite after fixing.

Days 2–4   Use the abbreviations at the top of the next page and the grammar cards to help you remember how to mark the passage. Your teacher will help you with anything you miss. Remember, a mistake is an opportunity to learn.

Of all the verbs you mark this week, decide which is the strongest and circle it.

Rewrite   Copy the corrected passage into a separate notebook.

- Be sure to double-space.
- Do not copy the markings, just the story.
- Be careful to indent where indicated and use capital letters properly.
- Carefully copy the punctuation and use end marks.

Page 18, *Fix It! Grammar:* The Nose Tree, Student Book 1

DAY 1

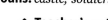

ar   *n*   *vb*   *ar*   *n*

Living at the **splendid** castle cheered the soldiers.

Fixes

End marks. Period at end of statement.

splendid: gorgeous; magnificent; dazzling

Grammar Notations

Nouns. *castle, soldiers.*

✏️ **Teacher's note.** The subject noun of this sentence is *Living* (*Living … cheered*), which is an unusual noun and not one most students will recognize, so it is not marked here. (See Grammar Glossary: Parts of Speech: Nouns: Noun Functions, page G-6, for more information on noun functions.)

Verbs. *cheered.* Explain the difference between a strong and a weak verb. Strong verbs give a powerful image or feeling or are more specific than weak ones.

Discuss with your students whether *cheered* is strong enough to count as a dress-up. Ask: Is *cheered* a strong verb? Does it give a strong image or mood or is it specific? Answer: Yes to both, so it counts as a strong verb dress-up.

Students may see this more clearly if you offer them a weak contrast. For example, compare "Living at the splendid castle cheered the soldiers" to "Living at the splendid castle was wonderful." "Cheered the soldiers" helps us see them at the castle in a cheerful mood. It is more specific and more colorful than the verb *was*, and it creates a vivid mood.

DAY 2

                                 pr   *vb*   *pr*   *vb*   *n*
    ¶ Soon, however, they decided they should not **dwell** at home always

            vb   *ar*   *n*
    but should explore the world.

Fixes

Indent. Start a new paragraph because of a new topic, their choice to leave.

End marks. Period at end of statement.

dwell: to live for a long time in a certain place

Grammar Notations

Verbs. *decided, dwell, explore.* See if your student can identify *they* as the subject of each of these verbs.

> Ask your students to vote on which they think is the strongest of these three verbs. There is not a right or wrong answer! *Decided* is stronger than *said. Dwell* works well because it implies staying somewhere permanently, which is more specific than *live. Explore* is stronger than *see* and explains why they want to travel.

DAY 3

                            pr   *n*   *pr* *vb*   *ar*   *n*
    Gathering ~~there~~/their ~~/they're~~ three gifts, they set out on a journey to visit

        ar   *n*
    a **neighboring** king.

Fixes

Homophones. Tell students to cross out the incorrect *there/their/they're* and check the spelling when copied.

End marks. Period at end of statement.

neighboring: living nearby

Grammar Notations

Verbs. *set.* If students mark *Gathering* or *visit* as a verb, praise them! See below.

> ♡ **Grammar lovers.** Some verbs include an adverb as part of the verb phrase, as in *set out*, which has a different meaning from *set* alone, but have students label only the verb.

> ♡ **Grammar lovers.** Verbals are words formed from a verb but not functioning as a verb. There are two verbals in this sentence, a participle (*gathering*) and an infinitive (*to visit*), both acting as adjectives here. Students do not need to learn these terms or be taught that some words that look like verbs are not actually verbs. The distinction is too advanced for this level.

✏ **Teacher's note.** For more information on verbals and infinitives, see page G-9 of the Grammar Glossary.

DAY 4

> *ar*   *n*   *n*   *ar* *n*   *vb*   *pr*
>
> Noticing the soldiers traveling in such **elegant** style, the king took them for
>
>   *n*
>
> noblemen.

Fixes

Indent. This could be considered a new topic (*the king's reaction*), but it is dealt with so briefly we do not have to start a new paragraph, arguing that it is on the same topic of their trip to the neighboring king. However, if your student prefers to start a new paragraph here, praise him!

End marks. Period at end of statement.

Grammar Notations

Nouns. *soldiers, style, king, noblemen. Style* is a noun because the sentence could have read "traveling in *the style* of elegance." *Noblemen* is a noun because it refers to people, it can be counted, and it could have *the* in front of it.

Verbs. *took.* Who took? (*the king*). Discuss with your student: Is it stronger to say "the king took them for noblemen" or "the king thought that they were noblemen"?

> ✧ **Advanced.** If students mark *Noticing* or *traveling* as verbs, praise them. These words are verbals (specifically, present participles) and do verb actions.

> ♡ **Grammar lovers.** The words *Noticing* and *traveling* are actually functioning as adjectives here, but the distinction is too advanced for this level.

elegant: tastefully fine and luxurious

✎ **Teacher's note.** See information in Grammar Glossary: Additional Rules and Concepts: Indentation Rules, page G-29, about beginning new paragraphs in fiction.

STUDENT REWRITE

Since this passage continues without another indentation, be sure students continue writing where last week's passage left off.

> Living at the splendid castle cheered the soldiers.
>
>   Soon, however, they decided they should not dwell at home always but should explore the world. Gathering their three gifts, they set out on a journey to visit a neighboring king. Noticing the soldiers traveling in such elegant style, the king took them for noblemen.

Week 9

Apostrophes to Show Ownership (Possessives)

LEARN IT

Apostrophes   This week you will learn how to use apostrophes to show ownership.

- If a part of the text is underlined, rearrange it to use an apostrophe-s to show what belongs to whom. For example, <u>the beautiful collar of the cat</u> should be changed to <u>the cat's beautiful collar</u>.
- Cross out the underlined text with a single line and write the new text in the space above.
- Use the new text in your rewrite, but do not underline it.

To help you remember these things for future lessons, add the Week 9 grammar card to your collection. Keep the remaining cards handy for review.

FIX IT

Read   Read the sentence.

Vocabulary   Look up the bolded word in a dictionary and decide which definition best fits the meaning of the word in this sentence. Add the definition to the list in the back of your notebook.

Day 1   Your teacher will help you mark and fix the first passage. Complete the rewrite after fixing.

Days 2–4   Use the abbreviations at the top of the next page and the grammar cards to help you remember how to mark the passage. Your teacher will help you with anything you miss. Remember, a mistake is an opportunity to learn.

Of all the verbs you mark this week, decide which is the strongest and circle it.

Rewrite   Copy the corrected passage into a separate notebook.

- Be sure to double-space.
- Do not copy the markings, just the story.
- Be careful to indent where indicated and use capital letters properly.
- Carefully copy the punctuation and use end marks.

Page 20, *Fix It! Grammar:* **The Nose Tree, Student Book 1**

Read the Learn It part with your students.

Adjust the lessons as needed.

This week students will be asked to use **apostrophes** to show ownership. This will not be demonstrated until Day 3.

Grammar Cards. Have your students find the new grammar card to add to their collection.

Once you have read the Learn It part, show your student how to apply it to the Day 1 passage.

✏ **Teacher's note.** Like quotation marks, true **apostrophes** are "curly," not straight — cat's, not cat's. Note that apostrophes always point downward. Many word processing programs have a "smart quotes" feature that will turn straight marks (' ") into curly ones (' ' " ") as you type, which usually works well.

DAY 1

    n   *vb* *ar*   *n*   *w-w* *vb*
¶ Now, this king had an only daughter, who was **crafty** as well as clever.

Fixes

Indent. Start a new paragraph because of a new topic, the daughter.

End marks. Period at end of statement.

crafty: skilled in underhand or evil schemes

Grammar Notations

Verbs. *had, was.*

> Strong verbs. Ask: Is either of these verbs strong enough to count as a dress-up? Answer: They are fine to use, but they are not very specific or colorful, so do not count such verbs as strong verb dress-ups.

> ♡ **Grammar lovers.** *Was* is technically a linking verb whose subject is *who* instead of an action verb, but this concept is advanced.

***Who-which* clauses.** Mark with *w-w* and read aloud: *who was crafty as well as clever.* Ask: What noun immediately before it does this *who* clause describe? Answer: *daughter.* Ask students to show you where the commas are placed. Answer: before the word *who* and after the whole clause.

✎ **Teacher's note.** Many students will not recognize that *be* verbs (*am, is, are, was, were, be, being, been*) are verbs. If your student misses *was,* simply point out that it is a verb. Model recognizing *be* words as verbs until your student can do this on his own.

DAY 2

      ar   *n*   *vb*   *n* *pr* *vb*
Because the princess could sense magical things, she became **observant** of

pr   *n*
her father's visitors.

Fixes

Apostrophes for ownership. *father's visitors.* Ask students if they can convert "her father's visitors" into a phrase beginning with "the visitors." Answer: the visitors of her father. Which sounds better? The original is less wordy: *her father's visitors.*

End marks. Period at end of statement.

observant: watchful; looking at attentively

Grammar Notations

Nouns. *princess, things, visitors.*

> ✦ **Advanced.** Possessive nouns like *father's* are nouns that function as adjectives. Confusing! Let students label *father's* as a noun or adjective or nothing.

Verbs. *sense, became.* Ask: Who or what is doing each of these actions? Answer: *princess could sense; she became.*

> ✦ **Advanced.** *Could* is a helping verb, which will be taught in the next lesson.

✎ **Teacher's note.** *Her* is sometimes a possessive pronoun, as here, and sometimes an objective pronoun, as in *they met her.* Students at this level do not need to learn how pronouns are used.

DAY 3

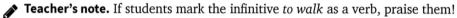
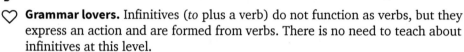

pr vb ar   *n*   *pr ar*   *n*

She invited the second soldier to walk with her in the **luxuriant** garden.

Fixes

luxuriant: abundant and beautiful in growth

Indent. Students might want to start a new paragraph since we turn to her walk in the garden with the second soldier, arguably a new topic, although the prior two sentences are brief enough and on topic enough to be in the same paragraph. Let your student decide!

End marks. Period at end of statement.

Grammar Notations

Verbs. *invited.* Ask: Who is doing this action? Answer: *She invited.*

✏ **Teacher's note.** If students mark the infinitive *to walk* as a verb, praise them!

♡ **Grammar lovers.** Infinitives (*to* plus a verb) do not function as verbs, but they express an action and are formed from verbs. There is no need to teach about infinitives at this level.

DAY 4

pr   vb   ar   n   pr   vb   ar

As they **roamed** under the flowering trees, she asked about ~~the splendid~~

n   ar   n

~~purse of~~ the soldier*'s splendid purse.*

Fixes

Apostrophes for ownership. This time, when students copy the passage into their notebook, ask them to convert "the splendid purse of the soldier" into a phrase without *of* and with an apostrophe: *the soldier's splendid purse.* Model this for students each time until they can do it on their own.

> ✎ **Teacher's note.** After students rewrite the possessive phrase in their notebook, the nouns will change. Since students mark the parts of speech on the student pages and not in the rewrite, have them mark the nouns prior to adding the apostrophe for ownership.

End marks. Period at end of statement.

> **roamed:** walked without a fixed direction

Grammar Notations

Verbs. *roamed* (who roamed? *they*), *asked* (who asked? *she*).

Strong verbs. Ask: Would *walked* have been a better verb choice than *roamed*? What about *wandered*? Note that both *roamed* and *wandered* are more specific and more colorful than *walked*, both suggesting aimless, pleasurable walking.

STUDENT REWRITE

Now, this king had an only daughter, who was crafty as well as clever. Because the princess could sense magical things, she became observant of her father's visitors. She invited the second soldier to walk with her in the luxuriant garden. As they roamed under the flowering trees, she asked about the soldier's splendid purse.

Week 10

Helping Verbs

LEARN IT

Verb (vb) In addition to action verbs, this week you will learn to identify helping verbs.

A helping verb is like a boy scout who helps an elderly lady cross the street. One always helps the other along! This week, mark helping verbs as well as action verbs with *vb* above each verb.

Helping verbs
- *am, is, are, was, were, be, being, been* (be verbs)
- *have, has, had*
- *do, does, did*
- *may, might, must, ought to*
- *would, will, could, can, should, shall*

Strong verbs On Day 4, decide which strong verb from this week's passages is the strongest.

To help you remember these things for future lessons, add the Week 10 grammar card to your collection. Keep the remaining cards handy for review.

FIX IT

Read Read the sentence.

Vocabulary Look up the bolded word in a dictionary and decide which definition best fits the meaning of the word in this sentence. Add the definition to the list in the back of your notebook.

Day 1 Your teacher will help you mark and fix the first passage. Complete the rewrite after fixing.

Days 2–4 Use the abbreviations at the top of the next page and the grammar cards to help you remember how to mark the passage. Your teacher will help you with anything you miss. Remember, a mistake is an opportunity to learn.

Of all the verbs you mark this week, decide which is the strongest and circle it.

Rewrite Copy the corrected passage into a separate notebook.
- Be sure to double-space.
- Do not copy the markings, just the story.
- Be careful to indent where indicated and use capital letters properly.
- Carefully copy the punctuation and use end marks.

Page 22, *Fix It! Grammar:* The Nose Tree, Student Book 1

Read the Learn It part with your students.

Adjust the lessons as needed.

This week students will identify **helping verbs**.

Grammar Cards. Have your students find the new grammar card to add to their collection.

Once you have read the Learn It part, show your student how to apply it to the Day 1 passage.

DAY 1

ar   n   vb ar   n   ar   n

The second soldier **rashly** told the princess about the purse.

Fixes

End marks. Period at end of statement.

rashly: hastily; without thinking

Grammar Notations

Verbs. *told* (who told? *The soldier*).

DAY 2

pr   vb   ar   n   vb   vb   vb   n

He **confided** that the purse was magical and would always refill with gold.

Fixes

End marks. Period at end of statement.

confided: told a secret or private matter

Grammar Notations

Verbs. *confided, was, would, refill.*

Ask: Which of these is the helping verb? Answer: *would,* which helps *refill.*

Ask students to identify the person or thing doing each action: *He confided; purse was; purse would refill.*

If your students overlook *was,* show them a list of the main *be* verbs (*am, is, are, was, were*) and ask them to find the one in this sentence.

DAY 3

> ar   n   w-w vb   vb   ar   n
> ¶ The princess, who was artful and **cunning**, formed a plan.

Fixes

cunning: full of deceit; sly

Indent. Start a new paragraph because of a new topic, the princess's scheme to steal the purse.

End marks. Period at end of statement.

Grammar Notations

Verbs. *was* (guide students to find the *be* verb), *formed*. Ask: What person or thing does the forming? Answer: *princess formed.*

***Who-which* clauses.** Ask students to read the clause aloud: *who was artful and cunning.*

Ask: What noun immediately before this *who* clause does it describe? Answer: *princess.*

Ask students to show you where the commas are placed.

DAY 4

pr vb   vb ar n   *the soldier's bag*

                                                    ar   n   ar

She set to work and made a purse **indistinguishable** from ~~the bag of the~~

  n   vb   vb   ar   n

~~soldier~~ so that no one would know one from the other**.**

Fixes

indistinguishable: identical; not to be told apart from

Apostrophes for ownership. In their rewrite ask students to convert "the bag of the soldier" into a phrase with a possessive apostrophe (*the soldier's bag*).

End marks. Period at end of statement.

Grammar Notations

Articles and nouns. *a purse, the bag, the soldier, the other.* If students do not catch *other*, remind them that the article *the* must be followed by a noun.

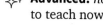 **Advanced.** *no one* and *one* are also pronouns, sometimes nouns, but not necessary to teach now if students did not mark them.

Verbs. *set, made, would know.*

Ask: Which of these is the helping verb? Answer: *would*, which helps *know*.

Ask: Who or what is doing each of the verb actions? Answer: *She set; she made; no one would know.*

Style

Strong verb dress-up. Instruct your students: Look back over all the action verbs from this week's passages and determine the one you think is strongest. Which dresses up the sentences best? Discuss their answer. Most likely candidate: *confided.*

STUDENT REWRITE

Since this passage continues without another indentation, be sure students continue writing where last week's passage left off.

The second soldier rashly told the princess about the purse. He confided that the purse was magical and would always refill with gold.

    The princess, who was artful and cunning, formed a plan. She set to work and made a purse indistinguishable from the soldier's bag so that no one would know one from the other.

Week 11

Read the Learn It part with your students.

Adjust the lessons as needed.

In addition to apostrophes for ownership, students will learn how to use **apostrophes to create contractions**.

Grammar Cards. Have your students find the new grammar card to add to their collection.

Once you have read the Learn It part, show your student how to apply it to the Day 2 passage since Day 1 does not have contractions.

Apostrophes with Contractions

LEARN IT

Apostrophes Continue to use apostrophes to show ownership by changing the underlined text. If the noun is plural (more than one), put the apostrophe after the *s*, for example, *cats' collars*.

Apostrophes can also be used for contractions where two words are combined into one by adding an apostrophe (') where letters have been left out, as in *wasn't* for *was not*. You will not have to create contractions this week; they are already there. Just notice them and be sure to put the apostrophe in the right place in your rewrite.

Contractions should not be used in reports, but they are permitted in story writing. Remember this in your own writing!

To help you remember these things for future lessons, add the Week 11 grammar card to your collection. Keep the remaining cards handy for review.

FIX IT

Read Read the sentence.

Vocabulary Look up the bolded word in a dictionary and decide which definition best fits the meaning of the word in this sentence. Add the definition to the list in the back of your notebook.

Day 1 Your teacher will help you mark and fix the first passage. Complete the rewrite after fixing.

Days 2–4 Use the abbreviations at the top of the next page and the grammar cards to help you remember how to mark the passage. Your teacher will help you with anything you miss. Remember, a mistake is an opportunity to learn.

Of all the verbs you mark this week, decide which is the strongest and circle it.

Rewrite Copy the corrected passage into a separate notebook.

- Be sure to double-space.
- Do not copy the markings, just the story.
- Be careful to indent where indicated and use capital letters properly.
- Carefully copy the punctuation and use end marks.

Page 24, *Fix It! Grammar:* **The Nose Tree, Student Book 1**

DAY 1

the soldiers' last night

      ar   *n*   *ar*   *n*   *ar*   *n*   *ar* *n*   *vb* *ar*

¶ On ~~the last night of the soldiers~~ at the palace, the princess held a

   n   *pr*

banquet for them.

Fixes

banquet: feast; lavish meal

Indent. Start a new paragraph because of a new time and a new topic, the plan carried out.

Apostrophes for ownership. Ask students to convert "the last night of the soldiers" into a phrase with a possessive apostrophe (*the soldiers' last night*). Model how to make a plural noun possessive by adding the apostrophe after the *s* instead of before. It is not one soldier's last night but the last night of all three soldiers.

End marks. Period at end of statement.

Grammar Notations

Verbs. *held*. Ask: Who held? Answer: *the princess held*.

✏ **Teacher's note.** When the noun is plural, form its possessive by writing the plural noun first (*soldiers*), then adding an apostrophe after the *s*.

DAY 2

      ar   *n*   *vb*   *vb*   *ar*   *n*   *vb*   *ar*   *n*

When the soldier wasn't looking, the princess **substituted** the magic purse

      ar   *pr* *vb* *vb*

for the one she had made.

Fixes

Apostrophes. Ask students to show you the contraction in this sentence and explain what it means: *wasn't*, contraction for *was not*. Ask: Do you know other examples of contractions? Show them a few common ones and/or have them write them out: *I'm (I am), I'll (I will), don't (do not), didn't (did not), isn't (is not)*.

End marks. Period at end of statement.

Grammar Notations

Nouns. If students flag *one* as a noun or pronoun, praise them, but you do not need to teach it at this level.

Verbs. *was* (part of the contraction *wasn't*) *looking, substituted, had made*. If they do not see the helping verbs, tell your students: There are two helping verbs in this sentence, one of them a little hidden. Can you find either?

✦ **Advanced.** Students may overlook *was* because it is a *be* verb and because it is merged with *not*. Simply point out to them that *was* is a helping verb, helping out *looking*.

substituted: traded or swapped one thing for another

✏ **Teacher's note.** If students wonder what *not* is, you can explain it is a different part of speech (an adverb because it modifies, or is added to, a verb).

DAY 3

<code>   ar   n   ar   n   vb   ar   n   vb</code>

¶ The next morning the soldiers **bade** the king **farewell** and headed

home.

Fixes

Indent. Start a new paragraph because of a new time and a new topic, their departure.

End marks. Period at end of statement.

bade farewell: told him goodbye (*bade* is the past tense of *bid*)

Grammar Notations

Verbs. *bade, headed.* Ask: Who is doing each of these actions? Answer: *the soldiers bade farewell; the soldiers headed home.*

Articles and nouns. *The morning, the soldiers, the king.*

- ✧ **Advanced.** If students mark *home* as a noun, praise them. It is actually an adverb here modifying the verb *headed,* but the distinction is unimportant and too advanced to teach at this level.

- ✧ **Advanced.** If students mark *farewell* as a noun, praise them. It is a noun in the expression "to bid farewell," but there is no need to teach it at this level.

DAY 4

pr   *vb*   *n*   *vb*   *n*   *ar* *n* *pr* *vb*

When they stopped for lunch and looked for gold in the purse, it **enclosed**

n   *n*

nothing but air.

Fixes

End marks. Period at end of statement.

enclosed: held or contained

Grammar Notations

Pronouns. *it.* Ask: What does *it* refer to? Answer: *the purse.*

Verbs. *stopped, looked, enclosed.* Who or what is doing these actions? Answer: *they stopped; they looked; the purse enclosed.*

Articles and nouns. *lunch, gold, the purse, nothing, air.*

✏ **Teacher's note.** Your students may have trouble recognizing some of these nouns. *Nothing* is countable because there are no things in nothing. It is also a thing, so it is a noun. *Air* and *lunch* could have an article in front of them, and *gold* is another thing, so these are all nouns. If your students do not grasp all of these, it is fine!

Style

Strong verb dress-up. Ask your students to choose the strongest verb from this week's sentences. Discuss their answer. Most likely candidates: *bade farewell* or *enclosed.*

STUDENT REWRITE

On the soldiers' last night at the palace, the princess held a banquet for them. When the soldier wasn't looking, the princess substituted the magic purse for the one she had made.

The next morning the soldiers bade the king farewell and headed home. When they stopped for lunch and looked for gold in the purse, it enclosed nothing but air.

Week 12

Indentation: When to Start New Paragraphs

LEARN IT

Indent

This week you will learn the reasons for starting new paragraphs and begin making choices about whether or not to indent.

In fiction (stories), you should start a new paragraph for these four reasons:

- new speaker
- new topic
- new place
- new time

In these fixes, add the ¶ symbol in front of sentences that should start a new paragraph. To make the symbol, just draw a backwards P with an extra line. You could also use an arrow (➜) in front of the sentence if that is easier for you. When you see that mark, remember to indent in your copy work.

To help you remember these things for future lessons, add the Week 12 grammar card to your collection. Keep the remaining cards handy for review.

FIX IT

Read

Read the sentence.

Vocabulary

Look up the bolded word in a dictionary and decide which definition best fits the meaning of the word in this sentence. Add the definition to the list in the back of your notebook.

Day 1

Your teacher will help you mark and fix the first passage. Complete the rewrite after fixing.

Days 2–4

Use the abbreviations at the top of the next page and the grammar cards to help you remember how to mark the passage. Your teacher will help you with anything you miss. Remember, a mistake is an opportunity to learn.

Of all the verbs you mark this week, decide which is the strongest and circle it.

Rewrite

Copy the corrected passage into a separate notebook.

- Be sure to double-space.
- Do not copy the markings, just the story.
- Be careful to indent where you indicated and use capital letters properly.
- Carefully copy the punctuation and use end marks.

Adjust the lessons as needed.

This week students will learn the rules of **indentation**. The passages will continue to be indented as needed, but the extra ¶ indicator will be missing. Have your students add it in where necessary to remind them to indent in their rewrite. You may let them use an arrow (➜) instead if desired.

Grammar Cards.
Have your students find the new grammar card to add to their collection.

Once you have read the Learn It part, show your student how to apply it to the Day 1 passage.

DAY 1

ar   *n*   *vb*   *pr vb*   *vb*   *ar* *n*   *ar* *n*

The second soldier remembered that he had **divulged** the story of the purse

ar   *n*

to the princess.

Fixes

divulged: told; revealed something private or previously unknown

Indent. In fiction (stories), we start a new paragraph for four reasons:
- new speaker
- new topic
- new place
- new time

Tell your students: Look at the last sentence you wrote last week. Do any of these four reasons for starting a new paragraph apply to today's sentence? Answer: No, the soldier's thoughts directly relate to the discovery that the purse is empty, so this is the same topic. The place and time have not changed, and no one is speaking. Continue writing where they left off and do not indent.

End marks. Period at end of statement.

Grammar Notations

Pronouns. *he.* Ask: To whom does the pronoun refer? Answer: *the second soldier.*

Verbs. *remembered, had divulged.* Ask: Who is doing each verb action? Answer: *second soldier remembered; he had divulged.* Ask: What is the helping verb? Answer: *had.*

♡ **Grammar lovers.** *had divulged* is a great example of the past perfect tense (*had* + verb), used when there are two different time frames in the past. The past perfect indicates an earlier time than the simple past.

DAY 2

pr   *vb*   *pr*   *vb*   *vb*   *pr ar n*

He **suspected** that she had played him a trick.

Fixes

suspected: believed likely

Indent. Is this a new topic, speaker, place, or time? Answer: No. We are still on the topic of the soldier's discovery of the empty purse and his response. No new speaker, time, or place.

End marks. Period at end of statement.

Grammar Notations

Verbs. *suspected, had played.* Ask: Who is doing these actions? Answer: *He* (the second soldier) *suspected; she* (the princess) *had played.*

DAY 3

¶   Immediately the first soldier threw his cloak across his shoulders and
ar   *n*   *vb*   *pr*   *n*   *pr*   *n*

wished himself in ~~the chamber of~~ the princess's *chamber*.
vb   *pr*   *ar*   *n*   *ar*   *n*

Fixes

chamber: private
room or bedroom

Indent. Is this a new topic, speaker, place, or time? Answer: Yes! We turn now to a new topic, the first soldier's action based on this discovery. In the middle of the sentence, he also travels to a new place. Check that your students marked the sentence with the indent symbol: ¶.

If your students want to argue about what constitutes a new topic, be flexible. It is often hard for them to see distinctions in topic; plus, some students love to argue. Since it is not critical that they agree on all topic choices, this is a great place to let them be right! The main thing is to get them to think about whether it is a new topic or some other reason for beginning a new paragraph.

For their rewrite, teach the rules for beginning a new paragraph: start on a new line and indent ½ inch.

Apostrophes for ownership. Have students convert "the chamber of the princess" into a phrase with an apostrophe. Answer: *the princess's chamber*. Ask: Which version is less wordy? Answer: The second.

This may confuse some students because the possessive of *princess* sounds identical to the plural of *princess*: *princess's* and *princesses*. For grammar lovers young and old, even stranger is the plural possessive: *princesses'*.

To add to the confusion, different grammar guides treat the possessives of nouns ending with *s* in different ways. *Chicago Manual of Style* (the style guide IEW uses) adds the apostrophe plus *s* to nouns ending in *s*.

End marks. Period at end of statement.

Grammar Notations

Verbs. *threw, wished.* Ask: Who is doing these actions? Answer: the first soldier does two actions: he both threw and wished. The same noun can have two or more verbs.

Pronouns. Students were not required to mark reflexive pronouns since there are not many in *Nose Tree*. If they labeled *himself,* praise them! If not, just explain that it is another kind of pronoun.

DAY 4

>   *pr   vb   pr*   *ar   n   pr vb*
> There ~~/Their/They're~~ he found her sitting alone, **tallying** the gold as it fell
>
>   *ar*   *n   pr   n*
> from ~~the wonderful purse of~~ his friend*'s wonderful purse.*

Fixes

tallying: counting; adding up

Indent. Is this a new topic, speaker, place, or time? Answer: No. We are still on the topic of what the first soldier does to remedy the loss. No new speaker, time, or place since he was already transported to her chamber in the previous sentence.

Homophones. Ask students to cross out the incorrect *There/Their/They're.* Check their spelling when copied.

Apostrophes for ownership. Rewrite: convert "the wonderful purse of his friend" into a phrase with a possessive apostrophe. Answer: *his friend's wonderful purse.*

End marks. Period at end of statement.

Grammar Notations

Pronouns. *he, her, it, his.* Ask: What noun does *it* refer back to? Answer: *the gold.*

Verbs. *found, fell.* Ask: Who or what is doing these actions? Answer: *he found; it (the gold) fell.*

✧ **Advanced.** If students mark *sitting* or *tallying* as a verb, praise them. Technically, *sitting* and *tallying* are verbals functioning as adjectives, but since they perform a verb action, it is fine if students count them as verbs.

Style

Strong verb dress-up. Ask your students to choose the strongest verb from this week's sentences. Discuss their answer. Possibilities: *divulged, suspected.*

STUDENT REWRITE

Since this passage continues without another indentation, be sure students continue writing where last week's passage left off.

> The second soldier remembered that he had divulged the story of the purse to the princess. He suspected that she had played him a trick.
>
> Immediately the first soldier threw his cloak across his shoulders and wished himself in the princess's chamber. There he found her sitting alone, tallying the gold as it fell from his friend's wonderful purse.

Week 13

Homophones, Exclamation Marks

LEARN IT

Homophones This week you will have the opportunity to identify the correct homophone in this trio: *to, two,* or *too.*

- *To* is the preposition, as in "to the window." It also begins phrases like "to spy."
- *Two* is the number 2. Notice that it has a double-u (w) in the middle. Double means two!
- *Too* means either "also" or "to an excessive degree" (too much). It is easy to remember because it has one too many o's!

End Marks You have already learned that every sentence must have an end mark. (. ? !)

This week you will have the opportunity to use an exclamation point (!). Use it at the end of an exclamatory statement (Stop that man!) or some interjections (Hey!).

To help you remember these things for future lessons, add the Week 13 grammar card to your collection. Keep the remaining cards handy for review.

FIX IT

Read Read the sentence.

Vocabulary Look up the bolded word in a dictionary and decide which definition best fits the meaning of the word in this sentence. Add the definition to the list in the back of your notebook.

Day 1 Your teacher will help you mark and fix the first passage. Complete the rewrite after fixing.

Days 2–4 Use the abbreviations at the top of the next page and the grammar cards to help you remember how to mark the passage. Your teacher will help you with anything you miss. Remember, a mistake is an opportunity to learn.

Of all the verbs you mark this week, decide which is the strongest and circle it.

Rewrite Copy the corrected passage into a separate notebook.

- Be sure to double-space.
- Do not copy the markings, just the story.
- Be careful to indent where you indicated and use capital letters properly.
- Carefully copy the punctuation and use end marks.

Read the Learn It part with your students.

Adjust the lessons as needed.

This week students will identify **exclamation points**, and a new homophone will be introduced.

Grammar Cards. Have your students find the new grammar card to add to their collection.

Once you have read the Learn It part, show your student how to apply it to the Day 1 passage.

Homophones: to. *To spy* is an infinitive, which does not act like other prepositional phrases. Starting with Week 19, students will be asked to mark prepositional phrases, but they will not need to identify infinitives.

DAY 1

          ar   *n*   *vb*   *ar*   *n*

Unluckily, however, the soldier **lingered** to ~~two~~ ~~too~~ spy on the princess

~~to~~ ~~two~~ too long.

Fixes

Indent. Is this a new topic, speaker, place, or time? Answer: No. The focus is still on the soldier, so students should continue writing where they left off last week.

Homophones. Ask your students to choose the correct *to/two/too* in each case and explain its meaning. Answer: the first is the preposition used with a verb, *to spy*. The second is *too* meaning excessively.

♡ **Grammar lovers.** *To spy* is an infinitive, a verbal (word formed from a verb but not functioning as a verb) formed from *to* plus the present form of the verb.

End marks. Period at end of statement.

lingered: delayed; stayed longer than needed

Grammar Notations

Verbs. *lingered.* Ask: Who is doing this action? Answer: *the soldier lingered.*

DAY 2

        pr   *vb*   *vb*   *pr*

¶   She **pivoted** around and spotted him.

Fixes

Indent. Is this a new topic, speaker, place, or time? Answer: Yes. Start a new paragraph because of a new topic, the princess's response. Check that students started on a new line and indented in their rewrite.

End marks. Period at end of statement.

pivoted: turned or whirled about on one foot

Grammar Notations

Pronouns. *She, him.* Ask: To whom do the pronouns refer? Answer: the princess and the soldier.

Verbs. *pivoted, spotted.* Ask: Who is doing these actions? Answer: She (the princess) is both pivoting and spotting.

DAY 3

                 ar   *n*   *pr*   *vb*   *n*   *n*

¶   **Rattled** for a moment only, she cried out with great force, "Thieves!

     n

Thieves!"

Fixes

Indent. Is this a new topic, speaker, place, or time? Answer: Yes. There is a new speaker. Explain that the paragraph begins at the beginning of the sentence, not at the quotations.

End marks. Use an exclamation point at end of an exclamatory statement or word.

Rewrite. Check that your students put the exclamation mark inside the closing quotations because it goes with what she says.

Grammar Notations

Verbs. *cried.* Ask: Who is doing this action? Answer: the princess (she) cried out.

♡   **Grammar lovers.** If students mark *Rattled* as a verb, praise them. It is actually functioning as an adjective describing *she*, but it expresses a verb action because it is a verbal.

rattled: confused; bewildered; disconcerted

DAY 4

              ar   *n*   *w-w*   *vb*   *pr*   *n*   *vb*

¶   The **ordinarily** bored courtiers, who heard her alarm, came running in

     vb   *pr*

and tried to seize him, ~~to / two /~~ too .

Fixes

Indent. Is this a new topic, speaker, place, or time? Answer: Yes. We turn to the response of the court and away from her speech, so this is a new topic.

Homophones. Have students cross out the incorrect *to/two/too*, explain the meaning of the correct word, and write it correctly in their rewrite. This one is *too* meaning also.

Spelling. Check that students spell *bored* and *seize* correctly in their rewrite. *Bored* has a homophone, *board*, which refers to planks of wood. *Bored* means uninterested; weary. *Seize* is one of the words that do not follow the usual "*i* before *e* except after *c* or when sounding like *a* as in *neighbor* or *weigh*" rule. Other common exceptions: *weird, their, either, height.*

End marks. Period at end of statement.

Continued on next page >

ordinarily: most of the time (that is, usually they are bored, but her cry prodded them into action)

Reading comprehension:

Courtiers are people who stay at court in attendance on the king or other royalty.

Seize means to grab or take by force.

Grammar Notations

Verbs. *heard, came.* Ask: Who is doing the actions *heard* and *came*? Answer: the courtiers. If students mark *running* or *seize* as a verb, praise them!

✦ **Advanced.** Because even grammarians will have different opinions about whether to treat the verbal *running* as part of the verb phrase *came running* or as a direct object of *came*, do not worry about it. It will not affect punctuation or effective communication to know! *Seize* is part of the infinitive "to seize" and not a true verb, but allow students at this level to mark verbals if they wish.

♡ **Grammar lovers.** Technically, *who* is the subject of *heard* because *who* or *which* is the subject of most *who-which* clauses, but accept *courtiers* as the answer.

Who-which clauses. Mark with *w-w* and read the clause aloud: *who heard her alarm.*

Ask: What noun immediately before it does this *who* clause describe? Answer: *courtiers.* Ask students to tell you where the commas are placed.

Style

Strong verb dress-up. Consider which is the strongest verb from this week's sentences. Discuss their answer. Best possibilities: *lingered, pivoted, spotted.*

STUDENT REWRITE

Since this passage continues without another indentation, be sure students continue writing where last week's passage left off.

Unluckily, however, the soldier lingered to spy on the princess too long.

She pivoted around and spotted him.

Rattled for a moment only, she cried out with great force, "Thieves! Thieves!"

The ordinarily bored courtiers, who heard her alarm, came running in and tried to seize him, too.

Week 14

Read the Learn It part with your students.

Adjust the lessons as needed.

This week students will identify **adjectives**. If you do not want to personify the pen for some of the adjectives, such as "the angry pen," then teach them to use this test: "the _____ pen or person."

Grammar Cards. Have your students find the new grammar card to add to their collection.

Once you have read the Learn It part, show your student how to apply it to the Day 1 passage.

Adjectives

LEARN IT

Adjectives (*adj*)

Adjectives are descriptive words that describe (or modify) nouns and pronouns. Usually they come before the noun they are describing (the *useful* pen), but they can come after a linking verb (it is *useful*). Write *adj* above adjectives.

To determine if a word is an adjective, apply this test:

- The _____ pen

To help you remember these things for future lessons, add the Week 14 grammar card to your collection. Keep the remaining cards handy for review.

FIX IT

Read

Read the sentence.

Vocabulary

Look up the bolded word in a dictionary and decide which definition best fits the meaning of the word in this sentence. Add the definition to the list in the back of your notebook.

Day 1

Your teacher will help you mark and fix the first passage. Complete the rewrite after fixing.

Days 2–4

Use the abbreviations at the top of the next page and the grammar cards to help you remember how to mark the passage. Your teacher will help you with anything you miss. Remember, a mistake is an opportunity to learn.

Of all the verbs you mark this week, decide which is the strongest and circle it.

Rewrite

Copy the corrected passage into a separate notebook.

- Be sure to double-space.
- Do not copy the markings, just the story.
- Be careful to indent where you indicated and use capital letters properly.
- Carefully copy the punctuation and use end marks.

Page 30, *Fix It! Grammar:* **The Nose Tree, Student Book 1**

DAY 1

> ar   adj   n   vb   pr   vb   n   ar
>
> ¶   The unfortunate soldier realized it was time to ~~two /too~~ **vacate** the
>
> adj   n
>
> crowded room.

Fixes

vacate: to leave a room or building

Indent. Is this a new topic, speaker, place, or time? Answer: Yes, a new topic, the soldier's flight, so start a new paragraph.

Homophones. Have students cross out the incorrect *to/two/too* and write the correct word in their rewrite.

    ♡ **Grammar lovers.** This is the preposition *to* in the infinitive *to vacate*.

End marks. Period at end of statement.

Grammar Notations

Pronouns. *it.*

    ✎ **Teacher's note.** If your student asks what *it* refers to, the answer is *time*, but a literal translation (*time was time*) does not make much sense.

Verbs. *realized, was.* If your students miss *was*, show them a list of the *be* verbs and ask them to find one: *am, is, are, was, were.*

    ♡ **Grammar lovers.** Verbals like infinitives (*to* plus the verb) are not technically verbs but show a verb action. It is fine if your students mark *to vacate* as a verb.

Adjectives. *unfortunate, crowded.* Ask: What nouns do these adjectives describe? Answer: unfortunate *soldier*; crowded *room*. Point out that these adjectives come immediately before the noun they describe.

DAY 2

	ar	adj	n	pr	vb	ar	n	vb	pr

Forgetting to use the magical cloak, he ran to the window, opened it, and

vb

vaulted out.

Fixes

vaulted: leaped or sprang

Indent. Is this a new topic, speaker, place, or time? Answer: No. Attention is still on the soldier and his need to escape.

End marks. Period at end of statement.

Grammar Notations

Pronouns. *he, it.* Ask: What does *it* refer to? Answer: the window.

Verbs. *ran, opened, vaulted.* Ask: Who is doing these actions? Answer: *he* (the soldier). If your students mark *forgetting* or *to use* as verbs, praise them.

♡ **Grammar lovers.** Verbals like this participle (-ing word) and infinitive (*to use*) are not technically verbs here but act like them since they show a verb action.

Adjectives. *magical.* Ask: What does this adjective describe? Answer: the cloak. Show that it comes right before *cloak*.

DAY 3

	pr	n	pr	n	vb	ar	adj	n	vb	vb

Regrettably, in his **haste**, his cloak caught on the rough sill and was left

behind.

Fixes

haste: hurry; rush

Indent. Is this a new topic, speaker, place, or time? Answer: No. Attention is still on the soldier's escape.

End marks. Period at end of statement.

Grammar Notations

Verbs. *caught, was left.* Ask: Who or what is doing these actions? Answer: His cloak does both actions: it caught and it was left.

Adjectives. *rough.* Ask: What does this adjective describe? Answer: the sill. Ask: Where do we find it? Answer: Right before the noun it describes.

DAY 4

<table>
<tr><td>ar</td><td>adj</td><td>n</td><td>vb</td><td>adj</td><td></td><td>pr</td><td>vb</td><td>ar</td><td>n</td><td>ar</td><td>n</td></tr>
</table>

The **covetous** princess was thrilled because she knew ~~the worth of~~ the cloak's

worth.

Fixes

covetous: wrongly desiring possessions

Indent. Is this a new topic, speaker, place, or time? Answer: This is a place where students may make their own choice about indenting. Some may argue it is a new topic since we turn to the princess's reaction. However, since it is short and still related enough to his hasty exit, it is fine to keep in the same paragraph.

Apostrophes for ownership. In their rewrite ask students to convert "the worth of the cloak" into a phrase with a possessive apostrophe. Answer: *the cloak's worth.*

End marks. Period at end of statement.

Grammar Notations

Verbs. *was, knew.* Ask: Who is doing these actions? Answer: *princess was, she knew.*

Adjectives. *covetous, thrilled.*

♡ **Grammar lovers.** Many students will not realize that *thrilled* is an adjective here. This is a subject complement following the linking verb *was.* See the information about subject complements in Grammar Glossary: Parts of Speech: Verbs: Linking Verbs, page G-8.

Style

Strong verb dress-up. Ask your students to choose the strongest verb from this week's sentences. Discuss their answer. Best possibility: *vaulted.*

STUDENT REWRITE

The unfortunate soldier realized it was time to vacate the crowded room. Forgetting to use the magical cloak, he ran to the window, opened it, and vaulted out. Regrettably, in his haste, his cloak caught on the rough sill and was left behind. The covetous princess was thrilled because she knew the cloak's worth.

Week 15

Read the Learn It part with your students.

Adjust the lessons as needed.

This week students will evaluate **adjectives**.

Once you have read the Learn It part, show your student how to apply it to the Day 1 passage.

Quality Adjective Dress-Up

LEARN IT

Adjectives (adj) As you label the adjectives, be on the lookout for *quality* adjectives. Like strong verbs, quality adjectives provide a strong image or feeling.

Reference your Week 14 card to remind you about adjectives.

FIX IT

Read Read the sentence.

Vocabulary Look up the bolded word in a dictionary and decide which definition best fits the meaning of the word in this sentence. Add the definition to the list in the back of your notebook.

Day 1 Your teacher will help you mark and fix the first passage. Complete the rewrite after fixing.

Days 2–4 Use the abbreviations at the top of the next page and the grammar cards to help you remember how to mark the passage. Your teacher will help you with anything you miss. Remember, a mistake is an opportunity to learn.

Look over this week's verbs and adjectives. Circle the single strongest verb and quality adjective from the week.

Rewrite Copy the corrected passage into a separate notebook.
- Be sure to double-space.
- Do not copy the markings, just the story.
- Be careful to indent where you indicated and use capital letters properly.
- Carefully copy the punctuation and use end marks.

Page 32, *Fix It! Grammar:* The Nose Tree, Student Book 1

DAY 1

          ar   *adj*   *n*   *vb*   *ar*   *adj*   *n*   *vb*   *pr*

¶   When the first soldier returned, the third soldier told him not

to ~~/two/too~~ **despair.**

Fixes

despair: give up hope

Indent. Is this a new topic, speaker, place, or time? Answer: Yes. Start a new paragraph because of a new place and time.

Homophones. Have students cross out the incorrect *to/two/too* and write the correct one in their rewrite.

♡ **Grammar lovers.** This is the preposition *to* in the infinitive *to despair*.

End marks. Period at end of statement.

Grammar Notations

Pronouns. *him.* Ask: To whom does this pronoun refer? Answer: the first soldier.

Verbs. *returned, told.* Ask: Who is doing these actions? Answer: the first soldier returned; the third soldier told.

♡ **Grammar lovers.** If students mark the infinitive *to despair* as a verb, praise them. These are not technically verbs but perform an action, so for now allow students to count them as verbs.

Adjectives. *first, third.*

Quality adjectives. Ask: Do any of these adjectives provide a strong image or feeling? Would you consider them quality adjectives, worthy of being counted as a dress-up? Answer: No. They are useful in distinguishing which soldier is intended, but they are not especially colorful or strong. These would not count as dress-ups in student writing.

DAY 2

pr   *vb*   *pr*   *adj*   *n*   *w-w*   *vb*

He blew his remarkable horn, which **vibrated** loudly.

Fixes

vibrated: produced a quivering sound; resounded

Indent. Is this a new topic, speaker, place, or time? Answer: No. This continues to show the third soldier's response.

End marks. Period at end of statement.

Grammar Notations

Pronouns. *He, his.* Ask: To whom do these pronouns refer? Answer: the third soldier. Point out that pronouns usually refer to the last noun (person if a *who* and object if a *which*) that agrees with them in number. Since *He* is singular, it must refer back to the last individual mentioned.

Verbs. *blew, vibrated.* Ask: Who or what is doing these actions? Answer: *He* (the soldier) *blew*; *which* (the horn) *vibrated*.

♡ **Grammar lovers.** *which* is the technical subject of *vibrated*, but it is fine if students explain that the horn is doing that action because it is!

Adjectives. *remarkable.* Ask: What does this adjective describe? Answer: horn.

Quality adjectives. Ask: Is *remarkable* a quality adjective? Does it give a specific image or mood? Is it a strong word? Answer: Yes! It reminds us that the horn has magical powers.

Who-which clause. Ask your students to read the whole clause aloud: *which vibrated loudly.* Ask: What noun immediately before it does this *which* clause describe? Answer: *horn.* Ask students to show you where the commas are placed—none at the end because this *which* clause ends the sentence.

DAY 3

ar adj n ar adj n n n vb ar n ar

At the first blast an **immense** troop of foot and horse rushed to ~~the aid of~~ the

n

soldiers' *aid.*

Fixes

Indent. Is this a new topic, speaker, place, or time? Answer: No. This shows what happened when he blew his horn.

Apostrophes for ownership. Ask students to convert "the aid of the soldiers" into a phrase with a possessive apostrophe: *the soldiers' aid.*

> Remind them how to make a plural noun possessive by adding the apostrophe after the *s* instead of before. It is not one soldier's aid but the aid of all three soldiers. Check that they do not write *soldiers's*, which is never right.

End marks. Period at end of statement.

Grammar Notations

Articles. Point out that *an* is used when it comes before a vowel sound. We would say "a troop" but "an immense troop."

Verbs. *rushed.* Ask: Who is doing these actions? Answer: troop. If your students answer "foot and horse" to this question, let it go.

♡ **Grammar lovers.** Technically it is the troop that rushed; *foot* and *horse* are objects of the preposition *of* describing *troop.*

Adjectives. *first, immense.* Ask: What do these adjectives describe? Answer: first blast; immense troop.

> Quality adjectives. Ask: Are these quality adjectives? Do they give a specific image or mood? Answer: *Immense* is a quality adjective; it draws our attention to the huge size of the army. *First* is not a quality adjective. While it is useful in helping us know that the result immediately followed the first sound of the horn, it does not create a vivid image or mood.

immense: huge; boundless

Explain that **foot** means foot soldiers or infantry.

DAY 4

ar	adj	n	vb		vb	ar	n	ar	n

The courageous soldiers set out and **besieged** ~~the castle of~~ the king*'s castle.*

Fixes

besieged: laid siege to; surrounded and attacked

Indent. Is this a new topic, speaker, place, or time? Answer: No, because it still discusses the results of the horn blast. If your students argue that it is a new topic because we are now addressing the soldiers, it is fine. Let them start a new paragraph, even though it will be quite short.

Apostrophes for ownership. In their rewrite ask students to convert "the castle of the king" into a phrase with a possessive apostrophe: *the king's castle.*

End marks. Period at end of statement.

Grammar Notations

Verbs. *set* (the verb phrase is *set out,* which has a different meaning from *set*), *besieged.* Ask: Who is doing these actions? Answer: the soldiers. Point out that the same subject, *soldiers,* does two verb actions.

 Advanced. Some students are confused by what look like prepositions after a verb but without the usual noun afterward. In this case, these words do not function as prepositions but as adverbs that must be coupled with that verb. Examples: the soldiers set *out,* the doctor chopped *up.*

Adjectives. *courageous.* Ask: What does this adjective describe? Answer: soldiers. Point out that *courageous* is hard to spell. Check that your students copy it correctly.

Quality adjectives. Ask: Is *courageous* a quality adjective? Does it give a specific image or mood? Is it a strong word? Answer: Yes!

Style

Have your students choose the single best of the following dress-ups from this week's sentences. Discuss their answers. Best possibilities:

Strong verbs. *vibrated, rushed, besieged.*

Quality adjectives. *remarkable, immense, courageous.*

STUDENT REWRITE

When the first soldier returned, the third soldier told him not to despair. He blew his remarkable horn, which vibrated loudly. At the first blast an immense troop of foot and horse rushed to the soldiers' aid. The courageous soldiers set out and besieged the king's castle.

Week 16

Read the Learn It part with your students.

Adjust the lessons as needed.

This week you will be discussing **capitals** and **contractions**.

Grammar Cards. Have your students find the new grammar card to add to their collection.

Once you have read the Learn It part, show your student how to apply it to the Day 1 passage.

✏ **Teacher's note.** The reason capital letters are called *uppercase* and minuscule letters are called *lowercase* comes from the days of hand typesetting. All of the letters were stored in shallow drawers, or cases, with many compartments for each letter. The upper case was for capital letters; the lower one was for minuscule letters.

Capitals and Contractions

LEARN IT

Capitals
Starting this week, you will not see any capital letters in the sentences. Follow the rules below to determine which words need to start with a capital letter.

- Use a capital letter for the first word of sentences, including the first word of quoted sentences.
- Use a capital letter for proper nouns such as names.
- Use capitals for titles like *king* and *princess* when used with a name but lowercase when they are not used with a name. E.g., *the king* versus *King Arthur*.

To show where capitals are needed, draw three short lines directly underneath letters that should be capitalized, like this: tom.

In your copy work, use capital letters where needed instead of those three lines.

Apostrophes
Continue to use apostrophes to show ownership and contractions. This week you can start creating your own contractions. For example, *did not* becomes *didn't*.

Cross out the underlined words and write the correct contraction above them. Be sure to use the contraction in your rewrite.

To help you remember the capitalization rules for future lessons, add the Week 16 grammar card to your collection. You can reference the Week 11 card to remind you of common contractions. Keep the rest of your grammar cards handy for review as you need them.

FIX IT

Read
Read the sentence.

Vocabulary
Look up the bolded word in a dictionary and decide which definition best fits the meaning of the word in this sentence. Add the definition to the list in the back of your notebook.

Day 1
Your teacher will help you mark and fix the first passage. Complete the rewrite after fixing.

Days 2–4
Use the abbreviations at the top of the next page and the grammar cards to help you remember how to mark the passage. Your teacher will help you with anything you miss. Remember, a mistake is an opportunity to learn.

Look over this week's verbs and adjectives. Circle the single strongest verb and quality adjective from the week

Rewrite
Copy the corrected passage into a separate notebook.
- Be sure to double-space and indent where indicated.
- Do not copy the markings, just the story.
- Be careful to use capital letters properly.
- Carefully copy the punctuation and use end marks.

Page 34, *Fix It! Grammar:* **The Nose Tree, Student Book 1**

DAY 1

didn't

| ar | n | vb | vb | | pr | vb | | vb | ar | n | | n | ar |

¶   the king was told that if he ~~did not~~ give up the purse and cloak, the

| n | vb | vb | vb |

castle would be **demolished**.

Fixes

demolished: destroyed; torn down

Indent. Is this a new topic, speaker, place, or time? Answer: Yes. Start a new paragraph because of a new topic, the king and his reaction.

Capitalization. Capitalize *The* because it is the first word of the sentence.

> If your students want to capitalize *king*, explain that titles are capitalized when they are used with a name (King Arthur). This is considered a common noun (lowercase), not a proper noun (capital), because there is no name.

Apostrophes. In their rewrite, have students form *did not* into its contraction *didn't*. Check that they put the apostrophe where letters are missing. Teach them that contractions work well in stories but usually not in formal papers.

End marks. Period at end of statement.

Grammar Notations

Verbs. *was told, did give, would be demolished.* If students mark *not* as part of the verb, point out that it is a different part of speech (adverb), not a verb at all.

✧ **Advanced.** If your students include *up* with *give*, praise them! Tell them they are right that *give up* with the adverb has a different meaning (to hand over or relinquish; to surrender) than *give* (to present to someone), but they only need to label the verb.

Ask: Who is doing these actions? Answer: *king was told; he* (king) *did* (not) *give up; castle would be demolished.*

Ask: Name the helping verbs in this sentence. Answer: *was, did, would be.* Remind students that helping verbs connect with action verbs to help them along (*was told; did give up; would be demolished*).

♡ **Grammar lovers.** *Demolished* may confuse some students. The verb is in the passive voice because the castle might be demolished by someone, so *demolished* is a verb and not a subject complement. See the information about passive voice and subject complements in Grammar Glossary: Parts of Speech: Verbs: Linking Verbs, page G-8, and Additional Rules and Concepts: Passive versus Active Voice, page G-33.

DAY 2

his daughter's chamber

ar	adj	n	vb	ar	n	pr	n		vb	pr

the weary king entered ~~the chamber of his daughter~~ and **challenged** her to

ar	adj	n

return the stolen treasures.

Fixes

challenged:
demanded as
something right to do

Indent. Is this a new topic, speaker, place, or time? Answer: Arguably. If your students want a new paragraph here on the basis of a new place, praise them! However, the events are brief enough and the focus still sufficiently on the king that we could keep it in the same paragraph.

Capitalization. Capitalize the first word of a sentence.

Apostrophes for ownership. In their rewrite ask students to convert "the chamber of his daughter" into a phrase with a possessive apostrophe: *his daughter's chamber*.

End marks. Period at end of statement.

Grammar Notations

Verbs. *entered, challenged.* Ask: Who is doing these actions? Answer: the king. Point out that the same subject (*king*) does two actions: he both enters and challenges.

♡ **Grammar lovers.** If students mark the infinitive *to return* as a verb, praise them. Infinitives such as *to return* are not technically verbs but perform an action, so for now allow students to count them as verbs.

Adjectives. *weary, stolen.* Ask: Who or what do these adjectives describe? Answer: *weary king; stolen treasures.*

DAY 3

I'll

pr	vb		pr	vb	vb			pr	adj	n

¶ she **countered**, "no! ~~i will~~ figure out how to trick them some way or

adj

another."

Fixes

Indent. Is this a new topic, speaker, place, or time? Answer: Yes. Start a new paragraph because of the new speaker. Teach that we start the paragraph at the beginning of the sentence, not in the middle where the speech actually begins.

Capitalization. Capitalize the first word of a sentence.

Teach: We also capitalize the first word of a quoted sentence (*No*), even when it falls in the middle of the full sentence.

Always capitalize *I* even when it is not the first word in a sentence. You might point out the oddity in our language that we capitalize *I* but not other personal pronouns.

Quotations. Remind students that spoken words are enclosed in quotation marks and that the period goes inside the closing quotation marks.

Apostrophes. In their rewrite, have students form *I will* into its contraction *I'll*. Check that they put the apostrophe where letters are missing.

End marks. Period at end of statement inside closing quotations.

Grammar Notations

Verbs. *countered, will figure* (*will* is part of the contraction *I'll*). Ask: Who is doing these actions? Answer: *She countered; I will figure out.*

Ask: What is the helping verb? Answer: *will*. Remind students that helping verbs connect with action verbs (*will figure out*).

✧ **Advanced.** This is another situation where the adverb (*out*) affects the meaning of the verb. *Figure out* (to solve or determine) has a different meaning from *figure* (to calculate or compute). Also, if your students count the infinitive *to trick* as a verb, praise them even though it is not technically a verb.

Adjectives. *some, another.*

✧ **Advanced.** Identifying these words as adjectives is advanced, so if your students do not, you can let it go. If you want, point out that both describe the noun *way* (some way or another way) and that adjectives describe nouns, so they have to be adjectives.

countered: to propose a contrary move or to reply with an alternative

This word is used as a verb (something she does), so it needs a verb definition, not one that fits a noun or adjective.

DAY 4

>   *ar*   *n*   *vb*   *ar* *adj*   *n*   *pr*
>
> ¶   t̲he princess thought of a cunning **ploy** to ~~two / too~~ outsmart them.

Fixes

ploy: a scheme or stratagem to gain an advantage

Indent. Is this a new topic, speaker, place, or time? Answer: Yes. Start a new paragraph because of a new topic, the actual plan. When a speech come to an end, consider what follows a new topic and start a new paragraph unless the following narrative directly points back to that speech.

Capitalization. Capitalize the first word of a sentence.

Homophones. Have students cross out the incorrect *to/two/too* and write the correct one in their rewrite.

    ♡ **Grammar lovers.** This is the preposition *to* in the infinitive *to outsmart*.

End marks. Period at end of statement.

Grammar Notations

Pronouns. *them*. Ask: To whom does this pronoun refer? Answer: the soldiers.

Style

Have your students choose the single best of the following dress-ups from this week's sentences. Discuss their answers. Best possibilities:

Strong verbs. *demolished, challenged, countered.*

Quality adjectives. *weary, stolen, cunning.*

STUDENT REWRITE

The king was told that if he didn't give up the purse and cloak, the castle would be demolished. The weary king entered his daughter's chamber and challenged her to return the stolen treasures.

She countered, "No! I'll figure out how to trick them some way or another."

The princess thought of a cunning ploy to outsmart them.

Week 17

-ly Adverbs

LEARN IT

-ly adverbs (*ly*) Many adverbs end in -ly. Look for them this week.

Notice the -ly adverbs in this sentence: "The *frightfully* covetous princess *completely* ignored her father." The first one (*frightfully*) modifies an adjective, and the second one (*completely*) modifies a verb.

Find the -ly adverbs and label them by printing a little *ly* over each one.

To help you remember the -ly adverb, add the Week 17 grammar card to your collection. Keep the rest of your grammar cards handy for review as you need them.

FIX IT

Read	Read the sentence.
Vocabulary	Look up the bolded word in a dictionary and decide which definition best fits the meaning of the word in this sentence. Add the definition to the list in the back of your notebook.
Day 1	Your teacher will help you mark and fix the first passage. Complete the rewrite after fixing.
Days 2–4	Use the abbreviations at the top of the next page and the grammar cards to help you remember how to mark the passage. Your teacher will help you with anything you miss. Remember, a mistake is an opportunity to learn.
	Look over this week's verbs and adjectives. Circle the single strongest verb and quality adjective from the week.
Rewrite	Copy the corrected passage into a separate notebook.

- Be sure to double-space and indent where indicated.
- Do not copy the markings, just the story.
- Remember to use capital letters properly.
- Carefully copy the punctuation and use end marks.

Read the Learn It part with your students.

Adjust the lessons as needed.

This week students will identify **-ly adverbs**.

Grammar Cards. Have your students find the new grammar card to add to their collection.

Once you have read the Learn It part, show your student how to apply it to the Day 1 passage.

✏ **Teacher's note.** Not all words that end with *-ly* are adverbs. Some common exceptions include *friendly, lonely, lively,* and *lovely*, which are all adjectives. If the word makes sense in front of "person" or "object" (*the friendly person, the lovely object*), it is an adjective, not an adverb. Only adverbs count as -ly words.

DAY 1

pr   ly   vb   pr   ar adj   n   ar   n   pr   n

s̲he cleverly **masqueraded** herself as a poor girl with a basket on her arm.

Fixes

masqueraded: disguised in a costume

Indent. Is this a new topic, speaker, place, or time? Answer: No. This sentence explains the plan referred to in the last sentence. Check that your students continue writing where they left off last week.

Capitalization. Capitalize the first word of a sentence.

End marks. Period at end of statement.

Grammar Notations

-ly adverbs. *cleverly*. Ask: What part of speech does this adverb describe? Answer: a verb, *masqueraded*.

Pronouns. If students labeled the reflexive pronoun *herself*, praise them! If not, just explain that it is another kind of pronoun.

DAY 2

n   pr   n   pr vb   ar   n   ar   n

s̲etting out by night with her maid, she **crept** into ~~the camp of~~ the enemy's

camp.

crept: approached slowly and quietly

Fixes

Indent. Is this a new topic, speaker, place, or time? Answer: Arguably yes because of the new location. However, this continues to show her plan in action, so it best belongs in the same paragraph.

Capitalization. Capitalize the first word of a sentence.

Apostrophes for ownership. In their rewrite ask students to convert "the camp of the enemy" into a phrase with a possessive apostrophe: *the enemy's camp.*

End marks. Period at end of statement.

Grammar Notations

Verbs. *crept*.

♡ **Grammar lovers.** If your students mark *setting out* as a verb, praise them. *Setting* is a present participle. Because it is a verbal (formed from a verb), it shows action but technically functions as an adjective, not a verb.

DAY 3

          n   *ly*   *pr*   *vb*   *pr*   *n*

<u>s</u>inging **ballads** charmingly, she soon drew from ~~there /~~ their ~~/ they're~~ tents

  ar   *n*   *w-w*   *ly*   *vb*   *ar*   *n*

the men, who gladly joined in the song.

Fixes

ballad: a simple song that tells a popular folk story

Indent. Is this a new topic, speaker, place, or time? Answer: No. This still shows her plan.

Capitalization. Capitalize the first word of a sentence.

Homophones. Have students cross out the incorrect *there/their/they're* and check the spelling when copied.

End marks. Period at end of statement.

Grammar Notations

Verbs. *drew, joined.*

> ✧ **Advanced.** Praise students who wish to mark *Singing* as a verb even though technically this verbal functions as an adjective. *To draw from* (to lure out of their tents) has a different meaning from *draw* alone.

-ly adverbs. *charmingly, gladly.* Ask: What part of speech does *gladly* describe? Answer: *joined,* the verb that comes right after it.

> ♡ **Grammar lovers.** *charmingly* modifies the verbal *Singing,* which functions as an adjective. Adverbs can modify adjectives, verbs, or other adverbs.

***Who-which* clauses.** Mark with *w-w* and read aloud: *who gladly joined in the song.*

Ask: What noun immediately before it does this *who* clause describe? Answer: *men.*

Ask students to show you where the commas are placed—again, no comma after the clause because it ends the sentence.

DAY 4

        ar   n   vb   adj   pr   adj   ar   n   ly

<u>while</u> the men were **preoccupied** with their own singing, the maid secretly

  vb   ar   adj   n

made off with the prized horn.

Fixes

Indent. Is this a new topic, speaker, place, or time? Answer: No. This still shows her plan.

Capitalization. Capitalize the first word of a sentence.

End marks. Period at end of statement.

preoccupied: distracted; completely occupied by their own thoughts

Grammar Notations

Articles and nouns. *the men, the maid, the horn.*

  ♡ **Grammar lovers.** *singing* functions as a noun, but few students of this age would catch it. This concept does not need to be taught now.

Verbs. *were, made.*

  ✦ **Advanced.** *Were* is a linking verb, linking the subject, *men*, to its complement, *preoccupied*. If students mark *preoccupied* as a verb instead, let it go. *Made off with* means stole, which has a different meaning from *made* (created).

Style

Have your students choose the single best of the following dress-ups from this week's sentences. Discuss their answers. Best possibilities:

Strong verbs. *masqueraded, crept.*

Quality adjectives. *preoccupied, prized.*

-ly adverbs. *cleverly, charmingly, gladly, secretly.*

STUDENT REWRITE

Since this passage continues without another indentation, be sure students continue writing where last week's passage left off.

She cleverly masqueraded herself as a poor girl with a basket on her arm. Setting out by night with her maid, she crept into the enemy's camp. Singing ballads charmingly, she soon drew from their tents the men, who gladly joined in the song. While the men were preoccupied with their own singing, the maid secretly made off with the prized horn.

Week 18

Read the Learn It part with your students.

Adjust the lessons as needed.

This week your students will differentiate between *its* and *it's*.

Grammar Cards. Have your students find the new grammar card to add to their collection.

Once you have read the Learn It part, show your student how to apply it to the Day 1 passage.

Its Versus It's

LEARN IT

Usage
It is easy to confuse *its* and *it's*.

Its refers to something belonging to *it*. Write it without an apostrophe.

it's

It's is the contraction meaning "it is." It is never correct to write the apostrophe after the *s*. To help you remember that *it's* = *it is*, write *it's* with a little *i* in the place of the apostrophe.

This week when you see the two options underlined, cross out the incorrect one and be sure to use the correct one in your rewrite. Continue to label both *it* and *its* with *pr* for pronoun.

To help you remember these things for future lessons, add the Week 18 grammar card to your collection. Keep the remaining cards handy for review.

FIX IT

Read
Read the sentence.

Vocabulary
Look up the bolded word in a dictionary and decide which definition best fits the meaning of the word in this sentence. Add the definition to the list in the back of your notebook.

Day 1
Your teacher will help you mark and fix the first passage. Complete the rewrite after fixing.

Days 2–4
Use the abbreviations at the top of the next page and the grammar cards to help you remember how to mark the passage. Your teacher will help you with anything you miss. Remember, a mistake is an opportunity to learn.

Continue to evaluate the dress-ups used this week. Out of all the choices, circle the single strongest verb, adjective, and -ly adverb from the week.

Rewrite
Copy the corrected passage into a separate notebook.

- Be sure to double-space and indent where indicated.
- Do not copy the markings, just the story.
- Remember to use capital letters properly.
- Carefully copy the punctuation and use end marks.

Page 38, *Fix It! Grammar:* The Nose Tree, Student Book 1

DAY 1

	ar	n	vb	ar	n	ar	adj	n	ly

¶ now that the princess had the horn, the besieging army instantly

vb		pr	n	vb	vb

disbanded and its, ~~it's~~ soldiers were sent away.

Fixes

disbanded: broke up; dissolved

Indent. Is this a new topic, speaker, place, or time? Answer: Yes. Start a new paragraph because of a new topic, the results of her theft.

Capitalization. Capitalize the first word of a sentence.

Usage. Tell your students to cross out the incorrect *its/it's*, explain the meaning of the correct one, and check the spelling when copied. Answer: *its* for the possessive form of *it*. Ask: What does *it* refer back to? Answer: the army. "Its soldiers" refers to the soldiers belonging to that army, or "the army's soldiers."

End marks. Period at end of statement.

Grammar Notations

Verbs. *had, disbanded, were sent*. Ask: What is the helping verb? Answer: *were* (were sent).

✧ **Advanced.** *Had* is often a helping verb, but here it is an action verb instead. Point out that there is no verb right after *had* for it to help along.

Adjectives. *besieging*.

✧ **Advanced.** If students do not label *besieging* as an adjective, it is fine to let it go. If they are curious, point out that it comes right before a noun and describes that noun, so it cannot be a verb in this sentence.

♡ **Grammar lovers.** See Grammar Glossary: Parts of Speech: Verbals, page G-9, for an explanation of the three functions of -ing words.

-ly adverbs. *instantly*. Ask: What part of speech does this adverb describe? Answer: the verb *disbanded*.

DAY 2

ar	adj	adj	n	vb	vb	ar	n	ar	n

the three **invaluable** gifts were left in the hands of the princess.

Fixes

Indent. Is this a new topic, speaker, place, or time? Answer: No.

Capitalization. Capitalize the first word of a sentence.

End marks. Period at end of statement.

invaluable: priceless; of value too great to be calculated

Grammar Notations

Articles and nouns. *The gifts, the hands, the princess.* Point out that often adjectives come in between articles and nouns, as in *The three invaluable gifts.*

Verbs. *were left.* Ask: What is the helping verb? Answer: *were* (were left).

DAY 3

ar	adj	n	vb	adj	adj		ar	adj	n	ar
the	three	soldiers	were	as penniless	and **forlorn**	as when	the	little	man	in the

adj	n	vb	pr	ar	n
red	jacket	found	them	in the	wood.

Fixes

forlorn: miserable; hopeless

Indent. Is this a new topic, speaker, place, or time? Answer: Arguably a new topic and therefore new paragraph because we turn to the soldiers. Again, it is short and sufficiently on the same topic, the consequences of her theft. Let students choose!

Capitalization. Capitalize the first word of a sentence.

End marks. Period at end of statement.

Grammar Notations

Pronouns. *them.* Ask: To whom does this pronoun refer? Answer: the soldiers. Point out that plural pronouns must refer back to plural nouns. Since *them* is plural and since *soldiers* is the most recently mentioned plural noun, *them* can only refer to *soldiers.* See Grammar Glossary: Parts of Speech: Pronouns, page G-7.

Verbs. *were, found.* If students ask whether *were* is a helping verb, it is not. It links the subject to the two adjectives describing *soldiers* so is a linking verb. Point out that there is no action verb right after it for it to help along.

Adjectives. *three, penniless, forlorn, little, red.* If students have trouble seeing that numbers can be adjectives, ask them to tell you what they describe. *Three* describes *soldiers,* which is a noun, and therefore *three* must be an adjective because only adjectives describe nouns.

✧ **Advanced.** Students may not recognize that *penniless* and *forlorn* are adjectives because they do not come right before a noun. Point out that they describe the soldiers.

♡ **Grammar lovers.** These are subject complements, which follow a linking verb (*were*) and describe the subject (*soldiers*).

DAY 4

              ly   *ar*   *adj*   *n*   *vb*   *pr*   *n*   *pr vb*

¶ **mournfully** the second soldier advised his friends, "~~its~~/it's ~~to/two/~~too

                       we'd

adj   *pr vb*   *vb pr*   *adj*   *n*

bad, but ~~we had~~ better go our separate ways."

Fixes

Indent. Is this a new topic, speaker, place, or time? Answer: Yes. Start a new paragraph because of a new speaker. Remind students that the paragraph begins at the start of the sentence, not at the quotation marks.

Capitalization. Capitalize the first word of a sentence.

> Also capitalize the first word of a quoted sentence even when it falls in the middle of the full sentence: … *friends, "It's too bad … ."*

Homophones. Tell your students to cross out the incorrect *its/it's*, explain the meaning of the correct one, and check the spelling when copied. Answer: *It's* for the contraction in *It's too bad*, meaning *It is too bad*. Have students cross out the incorrect *to/two/too*, explain the meaning of the correct one, and check the spelling when copied. This should be *too*, meaning excessively.

Apostrophes. In their rewrite, have students form *we had* into its contraction *we'd*. Remind them that contractions work well in stories, especially in dialogue, but usually not in formal papers.

End marks. Period at end of statement inside closing quotations.

mournfully:
sorrowfully; sadly

Grammar Notations

Adjectives. *second, bad, separate*. If your students do not recognize that *bad* is an adjective, let it go. Since *bad* modifies *it* and *it* describes the fact that follows (their need to part ways), it will be hard to explain why *bad* is an adjective.

> If your students mark *better* as an adjective, see the second advanced point under verbs below.

Verbs. *advised, is* (in the contraction *it's*), *had better go*.

> ✧ **Advanced.** If students ask, the subject of *is* in the contraction is *it*.

> ✧ **Advanced.** *had better* is an idiom (expression that does not make literal sense) meaning *ought to*. *Better* is part of this verb expression.

Pronouns. If your students do not label *our*, explain that it is another possessive pronoun but not in their list of pronouns to look for because this is its only appearance in *Nose Tree*.

Style

Have your students choose the single best of the following dress-ups from this week's sentences. Discuss their answers. Best possibilities:

Strong verbs. *disbanded, advised*

Quality adjectives. *besieging, invaluable, forlorn.*

-ly adverbs. *instantly, mournfully*

STUDENT REWRITE

Now that the princess had the horn, the besieging army instantly disbanded and its soldiers were sent away. The three invaluable gifts were left in the hands of the princess. The three soldiers were as penniless and forlorn as when the little man in the red jacket found them in the wood.

Mournfully the second soldier advised his friends, "It's too bad, but we'd better go our separate ways."

Week 19

Prepositions

LEARN IT

Prepositions (*prep*)

Prepositional phrases, such as *on the table*, *near the door*, and *over the mantle*, tell the position of something.

Prepositional phrases always begin with a preposition. To help you find them, use the list below, which is included on the Week 19 grammar card. Be sure to add that card to your collection.

Notice also that the prepositional phrase includes both a preposition and a noun, but no verb. To help you remember this, think "preposition + noun, no verb."

Whenever you see a preposition in the passage, write *prep* above it. To see the prepositional phrase better, underline the entire phrase like this:

<u>In the morning</u> the dog barked. The cat slept <u>under the table</u>.

Identifying prepositional phrases can be challenging, so if you find this difficult, your teacher can help you.

preposition + noun, no verb

aboard	at	despite	near	throughout
about	because of	down	of	to
above	before	during	off	toward
according to	behind	except	on, onto	under
across	below	for	opposite	underneath
after	beneath	from	out	unlike
against	beside	in	outside	until
along	besides	inside	over	unto
amid	between	instead of	past	up, upon
among	beyond	into	regarding	with
around	by	like	since	within
as	concerning	minus	through	without

FIX IT

Read — Read the sentence.

Vocabulary — Look up the bolded word in a dictionary and add the key word definition to your notebook.

Day 1 — Your teacher will help you mark and fix the first passage. Complete the rewrite after fixing.

Days 2–4 — Use the abbreviations at the top of the next page and the grammar cards to help you remember how to mark the passage. Your teacher will help you with anything you miss. Remember, a mistake is an opportunity to learn. Continue to evaluate the dress-ups used this week. Out of all the choices, circle the single strongest verb, adjective, and -ly adverb.

Rewrite — Copy the corrected passage into a separate notebook.
- Be sure to double-space, indent where indicated, and use capital letters properly.
- Do not copy the markings, just the story.
- Carefully copy the punctuation and use end marks.

Page 40, *Fix It! Grammar:* The Nose Tree, Student Book 1

DAY 1

ar   *adj*   *n*   *vb*   *ar*   *n*   *prep*   *ar*   *n*   *ar*   *adj*

¶ the second soldier took the path <u>to the right</u>, while the other·

n   *vb*   *prep*   *ar*   *n*   *prep*   *ar*   *n*

~~to~~/two ~~too~~ **determined** to travel together <u>down the road</u> <u>to the left</u>.

Fixes

determined: decided; resolved

Indent. Is this a new topic, speaker, place, or time? Answer: Yes. Start a new paragraph because of a new topic, pulling out of a speech and telling what the soldiers did.

Capitalization. Capitalize the first word of a sentence.

Homophones. Have students cross out the incorrect *to/two/too* and check the spelling when copied.

End marks. Period at end of statement.

Grammar Notations

Verbs. *took, determined.*

⭐ **Advanced.** It is fine if your students want to mark the infinitive *to travel* even though it is not technically a verb.

Adjectives. *second, other.*

⭐ **Advanced.** If your students do not mark *other*, you can let it go.

♡ **Grammar lovers.** In the phrase "the other two," the article *the* must point to a noun, which is *two* in this sentence. Note that if it had read "the two others," *two* would be the adjective and *others* the noun. However, this is too complex to teach most students at this level.

Prepositional phrases. *to the right, down the road, to the left.* Check that your students underlined each phrase starting with a preposition and ending with noun. Ask: What is the noun at the end of each prepositional phrase? Answers: *right, road, left.*

From your students' parts of speech notations, show that each phrase fits the prepositional phrase pattern (preposition + noun) and has no verb in it: *to … right; down … road; to … left.*

⭐ **Advanced.** The *to* in infinitives (*to* + verb) is a preposition, but since infinitives do not follow the usual prepositional phrase pattern, do not ask your students to mark *to* in them. If they do, you can explain that it is an exception from the usual prepositional phrase pattern and not to worry about it.

DAY 2

	ar	adj	n	vb		pr	vb	prep	ar	n
¶	the	second	soldier	**drifted**	until	he	came	to	a	wood.

Fixes

drifted: wandered without direction

Indent. Is this a new topic, speaker, place, or time? Answer: Yes. Start a new paragraph because of a new topic, the adventures of the second soldier.

Capitalization. Capitalize the first word of a sentence.

End marks. Period at end of statement.

Grammar Notations

Prepositional phrases. *to a wood.* Check that your students underlined the entire phrase.

Ask: What is the noun at the end of the prepositional phrase? Answer: *wood.*

From your students' parts of speech notations, show that the phrase fits the prepositional phrase pattern (preposition + noun) and has no verb in it.

DAY 3

adj   n   vb   ar   adj   pr   vb   vb   adj

<u>n</u>ow, this wood was the same one where they had met with so much good

n

fortune before.

Fixes

fortune: luck

Indent. Is this a new topic, speaker, place, or time? Answer: No. The sentence continues to talk about the wood mentioned in the sentence before.

Capitalization. Capitalize the first word of a sentence.

End marks. Period at end of statement.

Grammar Notations

Nouns. If students flag *one* as a noun or pronoun, praise them, but you do not need to teach it at this level.

Adjectives: *this, same, good*

✧ **Advanced.** Since the adjectives *this* and *same* are not descriptive adjectives, do not worry about it if your students cannot identify them correctly.

Verbs. *was, had met with.* Ask: What is the helping verb? Answer: *had,* which connects with *met.* If students answer *was,* praise them for recognizing that it is a verb. Point out that it is not a helping verb because there is no action verb right after it for it to join.

✧ **Advanced.** The verb phrase is *met with,* meaning *came across* or *encountered.* If students mark *with so much good fortune* as a prepositional phrase instead, it is fine to let it go since it does not affect punctuation or grammar.

♡ **Grammar lovers.** Here, *was* is a linking verb, linking the subject (*wood*) to the subject complement (*one*), a noun after the linking verb that renames the subject. Linking verbs are too advanced to teach at this level.

DAY 4

n   vb pr vb   adj   prep ar n   ly   vb

u̲when evening fell, he sat down **bone-weary** <u>beneath a tree</u> and promptly fell

asleep.

Fixes

bone-weary:
extremely tired

Indent. Is this a new topic, speaker, place, or time? Answer: Your students might argue that it is a new time. If so, it is fine to start a new paragraph here. However, doing so will place this sentence in a paragraph all by itself. It is enough on the same topic (the soldier's coming to the wood) that it can stay in the same paragraph.

Capitalization. Capitalize the first word of a sentence.

End marks. Period at end of statement.

Grammar Notations

Verbs. *fell, sat, fell.*

Adjectives. *bone-weary.* If students do not recognize this as an adjective, do not worry about it. It does not follow the usual pattern of coming before a noun. If they ask, tell them that it describes the pronoun *he* and that adjectives sometimes describe pronouns.

Prepositional phrases. *beneath a tree.* Check that your students underlined the entire phrase.

> Ask: What is the noun at the end of the prepositional phrase? Answer: *tree.*

> From their parts of speech notations, ask your students to show that the phrase fits the prepositional phrase pattern (preposition + noun) with no verb in it: *beneath … tree.*

Style

Have your students choose the single best of the following dress-ups from this week's sentences. Discuss their answers. Best possibilities:

Strong verbs. *determined, drifted.*

Quality adjectives. *bone-weary.* None of the other adjectives this week gives a strong image or feeling.

-ly adverbs. *promptly.*

STUDENT REWRITE

The second soldier took the path to the right, while the other two determined to travel together down the road to the left.

The second soldier drifted until he came to a wood. Now, this wood was the same one where they had met with so much good fortune before. When evening fell, he sat down bone-weary beneath a tree and promptly fell asleep.

Week 20

Discuss the Learn It part with your students.

Adjust the lessons as needed.

This week is review.

Grammar Cards. There are no new grammar cards for review weeks.

Review

LEARN IT

There are no new concepts for today. See if you can answer the questions below. If not, check your grammar cards for the answers.

- Name the three articles.
- What is the noun test?

Do you remember what these vocabulary words mean? If not, look them up in your vocabulary list in the back of your notebook.

- wretched
- rebuffing
- graciously
- dumbfounded
- wondrous

FIX IT

Read   Read the sentence.

Vocabulary   Look up the bolded word in a dictionary and decide which definition best fits the meaning of the word in this sentence. Add the definition to the list in the back of your notebook.

Day 1   Your teacher will help you mark and fix the first passage. Complete the rewrite after fixing.

Days 2–4   Use the abbreviations at the top of the next page and the grammar cards to help you remember how to mark the passage. Your teacher will help you with anything you miss. Remember, a mistake is an opportunity to learn.

                  Continue to evaluate the dress-ups used this week. Out of all the choices, circle the single strongest verb, adjective, and -ly adverb from the week.

Rewrite   Copy the corrected passage into a separate notebook.

- Be sure to double-space and indent where indicated.
- Do not copy the markings, just the story.
- Remember to use capital letters properly.
- Carefully copy the punctuation and use end marks.

Page 42, *Fix It! Grammar:* The Nose Tree, Student Book 1

DAY 1

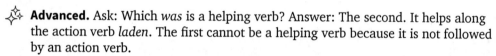

¶ <u>wh</u>en morning dawned, he was exceedingly delighted to notice that the

tree was **laden** <u>with the most appealing apples</u>.

Fixes

laden: loaded down; covered abundantly

Indent. Is this a new topic, speaker, place, or time? Answer: Yes. Start a new paragraph because of a new time.

Capitalization. Capitalize the first word of a sentence.

End marks. Period at end of statement.

Grammar Notations

Verbs. *dawned, was, was.*

> ✧ **Advanced.** Ask: Which *was* is a helping verb? Answer: The second. It helps along the action verb *laden*. The first cannot be a helping verb because it is not followed by an action verb.

> ✧ **Advanced.** If your students mark the infinitive *to notice* as a verb, accept it even though technically it is not a verb.

Adjectives. *delighted, laden, appealing.*

> ✧ **Advanced.** If your students do not recognize that these are adjectives, it is fine. You might point out that *appealing* comes just before a noun and describes it, which makes it an adjective. *Delighted* modifies *he*, which points back to the soldier, so it is also an adjective. *Laden* modifies *tree*, so it is an adjective.
>
> *Most* is sometimes an adjective, but only when it describes a noun, as in *the most apples*. Here, it describes the adjective *appealing* so has to be an adverb.

-ly adverbs. *exceedingly.* Ask: What part of speech does this adverb describe? Answer: an adjective. Teach that -ly adverbs can describe adjectives as well as verbs.

Prepositional phrases. *with the most appealing apples.* Check that your students underlined the entire phrase in rewrite.

> Ask: What is the noun at the end of the prepositional phrase? Answer: *apples*. Ask: How does the phrase fit the prepositional phrase pattern (preposition + noun, no verb)? Use the parts of speech notations to help show this. Answer: *with … apples* (and no verb).

DAY 2

pr   vb   adj   pr   vb   vb   adj   n
<u>h</u>e was hungry enough, so he soon **plucked** and feasted on several apples.

Fixes

plucked: picked; pulled with a sudden jerk

Indent. Is this a new topic, speaker, place, or time? Answer: No, because the topic of the apples has not changed; continue writing in the same paragraph.

Capitalization. Capitalize the first word of a sentence.

End marks. Period at end of statement.

Grammar Notations

Verbs. *was, plucked, feasted on* (*on* goes with the verb). Show that two verbs have the same subject, the second *he*: *he … plucked and feasted on.*

> ✧ **Advanced.** If students mark *on several apples* as a prepositional phrase instead, it is fine.

Adjectives. *hungry, several.*

> ✧ **Advanced.** *hungry* is another adjective that comes after the noun or pronoun it describes.

> ♡ **Grammar lovers.** *was* is another linking verb linking *he* to the subject complement *hungry.*

DAY 3

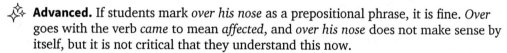

ar | adj | | n | vb | | pr | n | w-w | vb | | vb | pr

<u>a</u> **peculiar** feeling came over his nose, which had never troubled him before.

Fixes

peculiar: strange; odd

Indent. Is this a new topic, speaker, place, or time? Answer: No, this is the same topic about the apples.

Capitalization. Capitalize the first word of a sentence.

End marks. Period at end of statement.

Grammar Notations

Verbs. *came, had troubled.* Ask: What is the helping verb? Answer: *had,* because it helps *troubled* along.

> ✧ **Advanced.** If students mark *over his nose* as a prepositional phrase, it is fine. *Over* goes with the verb *came* to mean *affected,* and *over his nose* does not make sense by itself, but it is not critical that they understand this now.

Who-which clauses. Mark with *w-w* and read aloud: *which had never troubled him before.*

Ask: What noun immediately before it does this *which* clause describe? Answer: *nose.*

Ask students to show you where the commas are placed (just before *which*).

DAY 4

pr   *vb*   *pr*   *vb*   *ly*   *vb*
h̲e **detected** that it was rapidly growing.

Fixes

detected: discovered; found out

Indent. Is this a new topic, speaker, place, or time? Answer: No, this is the same topic about the result of eating the apples.

Capitalization. Capitalize the first word of a sentence.

End marks. Period at end of statement.

Grammar Notations

Pronouns. *He, it.* Ask: What does *it* refer back to? Answer: his nose.

Verbs. *detected, was growing.* Ask: What is the helping verb? Answer: *was,* which helps *growing.*

-ly adverbs. *rapidly.* Ask: What part of speech does this adverb describe? Answer: the verb *growing.*

Style

Have your students choose the single best of the following dress-ups from this week's sentences. Discuss their answers. Best possibilities:

Strong verbs. *dawned, laden, plucked, feasted,* all of which give a colorful image or feeling.

Quality adjectives. *appealing, peculiar.*

-ly adverbs. *exceedingly, rapidly.*

 Institute for Excellence in Writing

STUDENT REWRITE

When morning dawned, he was exceedingly delighted to notice that the tree was laden with the most appealing apples. He was hungry enough, so he soon plucked and feasted on several apples. A peculiar feeling came over his nose, which had never troubled him before. He detected that it was rapidly growing.

Week 21

Read the Learn It part with your students.

Adjust the lessons as needed.

This week students will identify **coordinating conjunctions**.

Grammar Cards. Have your students find the new grammar card to add to their collection.

Once you have read the Learn It part, show your student how to apply it to the Day 1 passage.

Coordinating Conjunctions

LEARN IT

Coordinating Conjunctions (*cc*)

Grammarians give names to different kinds of words. The names they choose can look frightening at first, but after saying them a few times they are not so bad.

This week you will learn to identify coordinating conjunctions. *Coordinating* means the words match; they are the same types. *Conjunction* means that two or more things are joined together. Thus, coordinating conjunctions connect together two or more of the same types of words, phrases, or clauses.

The coordinating conjunctions (*cc* for short) are easy to identify. There are seven of them: *for, and, nor, but, or, yet, so.*

An easy way to remember the list is to learn the acronym, FANBOYS. An acronym is a word formed from the first letters of other words, in this case, the coordinating conjunctions.

To help you remember the list of coordinating conjunctions (FANBOYS), add the Week 21 grammar card to your collection. Keep the rest of your grammar cards handy for review as you need them.

FIX IT

Read
Read the sentence.

Vocabulary
Look up the bolded word in a dictionary and add the key word definition to your notebook.

Day 1
Your teacher will help you mark and fix the first passage. Complete the rewrite after fixing.

Days 2–4
Use the abbreviations at the top of the next page and the grammar cards to help you remember how to mark the passage. Your teacher will help you with anything you miss. Remember, a mistake is an opportunity to learn.

Continue to evaluate the dress-ups used this week. Out of all the choices, circle the single strongest verb, adjective, and -ly adverb from the week.

Rewrite
Copy the corrected passage into a separate notebook.

- Be sure to double-space and indent where indicated.
- Do not copy the markings, just the story.
- Remember to use capital letters properly.
- Carefully copy the punctuation and use end marks.

Page 44, *Fix It! Grammar:* **The Nose Tree, Student Book 1**

DAY 1

pr   *pr*   *vb*   *pr vb*   *ly*   *vb*   *cc*   *vb*

¶   "dear me!" he exclaimed. "~~its~~/it's steadily changing and growing! when

vb   *pr*   *vb*

will it **cease?**"

Fixes

cease: stop

Indent. Is this a new topic, speaker, place, or time? Answer: Yes. Start a new paragraph because of a new speaker.

Capitalization. Capitalize the first word of quoted sentences: *Dear, It's, When.* (Also, see the first advanced notation under Punctuation.)

Usage. Have students cross out the incorrect *its/it's,* explain the meaning of the correct word, and check the spelling when copied. This should be *It's* for the contraction: *It is* steadily growing, or *It's* steadily growing.

Punctuation. Guide students to add an exclamation mark after "Dear me" because it is something the soldier exclaims. The exclamation mark goes inside the closing quotations because it is part of his speech.

✦ **Advanced.** Speaking verbs and their subject (*he exclaimed*) that set up quotations (*"Dear me!"*) are part of the same sentence as the quotation, so *he* is lowercase even though it follows an end mark.

✦ **Advanced.** Often there is more than one way to punctuate a sentence. This sentence could instead be punctuated like this: *"Dear me," he exclaimed. "it's steadily changing and growing!"* In this case, *"Dear me"* is part of the same sentence as *"it's steadily changing and growing!"*

End marks. Use a question mark at the end of his question. Check that students place it inside the closing quotation marks because it goes with his words.

Grammar Notations

Verbs. *exclaimed, is* (in *it's*) *growing, will cease.* Ask: Which of these are helping verbs? Answer: *is,* which helps *growing* along; *will,* which helps *cease.*

-ly adverbs. *steadily.* Ask: What part of speech does this -ly adverb describe? Answer: the verb *growing.*

Coordinating conjunctions. Ask: What does the cc *and* join? Answer: *changing* and *growing.* Ask: Are these the same part of speech? Answer: Yes. Explain that there is no comma before the cc because it joins only two verbs, not three or more.

DAY 2

vb   pr   vb   cc   prep   adj   n   pr   vb   prep   ar   n   pr   vb   prep

¶   well might he ask, for <u>by this time</u> it **arched** <u>to the ground</u> as he sat <u>on</u>

ar   adj   n

<u>the damp grass.</u>

Fixes

Indent. Is this a new topic, speaker, place, or time? Answer: Yes. Start a new paragraph because of a new topic, pulling out of his speech and telling about the nose.

Capitalization. Capitalize the first word of a sentence.

End marks. Period at end of statement.

arched: stretched out in the shape of an arch or something curved

Grammar Notations

Pronouns. *he, it, he.* Ask: What does *it* refer to? Answer: his nose.

Verbs. *might ask, arched, sat.* Ask: Which of these are helping verbs? Answer: *might*, which helps along *ask*.

Prepositional phrases. *by this time, to the ground, on the grass.* Check that your students underlined the entire phrases in their rewrite.

Ask: What is the noun at the end of each prepositional phrase? Answer: *time, ground, grass.*

Ask: How does the phrase fit the pattern (preposition + noun, no verb)? Use the parts of speech notations to help show this. Answer: *by … time; to … ground; on grass.*

Coordinating conjunctions. *for.*

✧ **Advanced.** This cc joins two main clauses (*Well might he ask* and *it arched to the ground*), which requires a comma before the cc. Pattern: **MC, cc MC**.

DAY 3

<u>it</u> continued to **inch on** until he could not bear its ~~it's~~ weight or raise himself

up.

Fixes

inch on: move by inches or small degrees

Indent. Is this a new topic, speaker, place, or time? Answer: No, because the sentence continues to develop the topic of his growing nose.

Capitalization. Capitalize the first word of a sentence.

Usage. Have students cross out the incorrect *its/it's*, explain the meaning of the correct one, and check the spelling when copied. This should be *its* expressing possession or ownership: the weight of the nose, or its weight.

End marks. Period at end of statement.

Grammar Notations

Pronouns. *It, he, its, himself*. Ask: What does *it* refer to? Answer: his nose.

If students labeled the reflexive pronoun *himself*, praise them! If not, just explain that it is another kind of pronoun.

Verbs. *continued, could bear, raise* (*up* is an adverb here that goes with this verb).

Ask: Which of these are helping verbs? Answer: could.

If students mark the infinitive *to inch on* as a verb, it is fine.

Coordinating conjunctions. *or.*

✧ **Advanced.** Explain that cc's must connect words that are the same part of speech. Here, *or* joins two verbs: *could bear ... or raise*. Use the part of speech notation to guide students to see this.

DAY 4

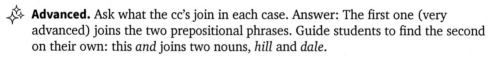

| pr | vb | pr | adj | n | prep | ar | n | cc | prep |

already it stretched its/~~it's~~ enormous length all <u>through the wood</u> and <u>over</u>

| n | cc | n |

<u>hill and **dale.**</u>

Fixes

dale: an open valley

Indent. Is this a new topic, speaker, place, or time? Answer: No, because the sentence continues to talk about his growing nose.

Capitalization. Capitalize the first word of a sentence.

Usage. Tell students to cross out the incorrect *its/it's*, explain the meaning of the correct one, and check the spelling when copied. This should be *its* expressing possession: the length of the nose, or its length.

End marks. Period at end of statement.

Grammar Notations

Pronouns. *it, its*. Ask: What does *it* refer to? Answer: the soldier's nose.

Prepositional phrases. *through the wood, over hill and dale.*

Ask: What is the noun at the end of each prepositional phrase? Answer: *wood, hill … dale* (two nouns).

Ask: How does each phrase fit the pattern (preposition + noun, no verb)? Use the parts of speech notations to help show this. Answer: *through … wood; over … hill … dale.*

Coordinating conjunctions. *and, and.*

✧ **Advanced.** Ask what the cc's join in each case. Answer: The first one (very advanced) joins the two prepositional phrases. Guide students to find the second on their own: this *and* joins two nouns, *hill* and *dale.*

Style

Have your students choose the single best of the following dress-ups from this week's sentences. Discuss their answers. Best possibilities:

Strong verbs. *cease, arched, stretched*

Quality adjectives. *damp, enormous*

-ly adverbs. *steadily* since it is the only one.

STUDENT REWRITE

"Dear me!" he exclaimed. "It's steadily changing and growing! When will it cease?"

Well might he ask, for by this time it arched to the ground as he sat on the damp grass. It continued to inch on until he could not bear its weight or raise himself up. Already it stretched its enormous length all through the wood and over hill and dale.

Week 22

Discuss the Learn It part with your students.

Adjust the lessons as needed.

This week is a review week.

Review

LEARN IT

There are no new concepts for today. See if you can answer the questions below. If not, check your grammar cards for the answers.

- What is a test for verbs?
- Can you list the coordinating conjunctions? (Hint: FANBOYS)

Do you remember what these vocabulary words mean? If not, look them up in your vocabulary list in the back of your notebook.

- abundant
- curious
- sociable
- survey
- splendid

FIX IT

Read	Read the sentence.
Vocabulary	Look up the bolded word in a dictionary and decide which definition best fits the meaning of the word in this sentence. Add the definition to the list in the back of your notebook.
Day 1	Your teacher will help you mark and fix the first passage. Complete the rewrite after fixing.
Days 2–4	Use the abbreviations at the top of the next page and the grammar cards to help you remember how to mark the passage. Your teacher will help you with anything you miss. Remember, a mistake is an opportunity to learn. Continue to evaluate the dress-ups used this week. Out of all the choices, circle the single strongest verb, adjective, and -ly adverb from the week.
Rewrite	Copy the corrected passage into a separate notebook. ▪ Be sure to double-space and indent where indicated. ▪ Do not copy the markings, just the story. ▪ Remember to use capital letters properly. ▪ Carefully copy the punctuation and use end marks.

Page 46, *Fix It! Grammar:* The Nose Tree, Student Book 1

Institute for Excellence in Writing

DAY 1

¶   ^{pr} ⁿ ^{w-w} ^{vb} ^{pr} ⁿ

¶   __meantime__, his comrades, who continued ~~there/~~their~~/they're~~ journey,

^{vb} ^{prep} ^{adj} ^{adj} ⁿ

came to that same wood.

Fixes

Indent. Is this a new topic, speaker, place, or time? Answer: Yes. Start a new paragraph because of a new place.

Capitalization. Capitalize the first word of a sentence.

Homophones. Have students cross out the incorrect *there/their/they're* and check the spelling when copied.

End marks. Period at end of statement.

meantime: meanwhile; at the same time

Grammar Notations

Adjectives. *that, same.*

 Advanced. If your students do not mark these, let it go. Since they are not descriptive, it will be hard for many students to recognize that these are adjectives. Optional: Point out that both words describe the noun *wood* (*that wood; same wood*), and only adjectives can describe nouns.

Prepositional phrases. *to that same wood.*

Ask: What is the noun at the end of the prepositional phrase? Answer: *wood.*

Ask: How does the phrase fit the pattern (preposition + noun, no verb)? Use the parts of speech notations to help show this. Answer: *to … wood.*

Who-which clauses. Mark with *w-w* and read aloud: *who continued their journey.*

Ask: What noun immediately before it does this *who* clause describe? Answer: *comrades.*

Ask students to show you where the commas are placed.

 Advanced. Point out that the *who* clause has its own verb (*who were journeying*) and that there must be another verb in the sentence that is not inside the *who* clause: *his comrades came.* Tell them Mr. Pudewa's words: "Don't let your *who* clause steal your sentence!"

DAY 2

ly		prep	pr	vb	prep	n	adj

suddenly, one of them stumbled over something **bizarre.**

Fixes

bizarre: unusual; strange; unexpected

Indent. Is this a new topic, speaker, place, or time? Answer: No, because it continues the topic of their travel in the wood.

Capitalization. Capitalize the first word of a sentence.

End marks. Period at end of statement.

Grammar notations

Nouns. If students flag *one* as a noun or pronoun, praise them, but you do not need to teach it at this level.

Adjectives. *bizarre*. Ask: What does *bizarre* describe? Answer: *something*. Adjectives can modify pronouns as well as nouns.

Prepositional phrases. *of them, over something.*

Explain that prepositional phrases can end in nouns or pronouns. Ask: What is the noun or pronoun at the end of each prepositional phrase? Answer: *them, something.*

Ask: How does the phrase fit the pattern (preposition + noun/pronoun, no verb)? Use the parts of speech notations to help show this.

DAY 3

vb   vb   vb   ar   n   pr vb   ar   n   cc   n

¶ "what can that be?" **queried** the other. "~~its~~ it's not a tree root or stump."

Fixes

queried: asked

Indent. Is this a new topic, speaker, place, or time? Answer: Yes. Start a new paragraph because of a new speaker.

Capitalization. Capitalize the first word of a sentence (*What*) and of a quoted sentence (*It's*).

Usage. Have students cross out the incorrect *its/it's*, explain the meaning of the correct one, and check the spelling when copied. This should be *It's* for the contraction: *It is* not a tree root, or *It's* not a tree root.

Punctuation. Use a question mark inside the quotes since he is asking a question.

⟡ **Advanced.** The first quotation is followed by a lowercase word since "queried the other" sets up the quotation and is part of that same sentence even though it follows an end mark.

End marks. Period at end of statement inside closing quotation marks.

Grammar Notations

Pronouns. *it.*

⟡ **Advanced.** *that* is also a pronoun here.

Verbs. *can be, queried, is* (in *it's*).

Coordinating conjunctions. *or.*

    Ask: What words does this cc join? Answer: *tree root* and *stump.*

DAY 4

           pr   *ly*   *vb*   *ar* *adj*   *n*   *cc*   *vb*   *vb* *prep*   *n*   *pr*

¶ they carefully **inspected** the odd thing and could think <u>of nothing</u> that it

       vb   *cc* *ar* *n*

resembled but a nose**.**

Fixes

inspected: looked carefully at; examined

Indent. Is this a new topic, speaker, place, or time? Answer: Yes. Start a new paragraph because of a new topic, pulling out of a speech and turning to their inspection.

Capitalization. Capitalize the first word of a sentence.

End marks. Period at end of statement.

Grammar Notations

Pronouns. *They, it.* Ask: What does *it* refer to? Answer: the thing they stumbled over, his nose.

-ly adverbs. *carefully*. Ask: What part of speech does this adverb describe? Answer: the verb *inspected*.

Prepositional phrases. *of nothing*. Ask: How does the phrase fit the pattern (preposition + noun, no verb)? Use the parts of speech notations to help show this.

Coordinating conjunctions. *and, but.*

   ⬩ **Advanced.** Ask what words these cc's join. Answer: *and* joins two verbs (*inspected* and *could think*) to the same subject (*they*); *but* joins two nouns, *nothing* and *nose*.

   ✎ **Teacher's note.** To be grammatical, coordinating conjunctions must join the same parts of speech.

Style

Have your students choose the single best of the following dress-ups from this week's sentences. Discuss their answers. Best possibilities:

Strong verbs. *stumbled, queried, inspected, resembled.*

Quality adjectives. *bizarre, odd.*

-ly adverbs. *suddenly, carefully.*

STUDENT REWRITE

Meantime, his comrades, who continued their journey, came to that same wood. Suddenly, one of them stumbled over something bizarre.

"What can that be?" queried the other. "It's not a tree root or stump."

They carefully inspected the odd thing and could think of nothing that it resembled but a nose.

Week 23

Read the Learn It part with your students.

Adjust the lessons as needed.

This week students will identify **clause starters**.

Grammar Cards. Have your students find the new grammar card to add to their collection.

Once you have read the Learn It part, show your student how to apply it to the Day 1 passage.

Clause Starters

LEARN IT

Clause starters: when, while, where, as, since, if, although, because

Another dress-up provides a new list of words: *when, while, where, as, since, if, although, because*. There is even an acronym to help you remember the list: *www.asia.b*. Easy!

These clause starters usually begin an adverb clause, but all you need to do is remember the list. There are more words that could be added to the list, but this one will get you started.

If you really want to sound smart, you can learn what these words are called by grammarians: *subordinating conjunctions*. But you do not need to worry about that term. Just learn the list of words: *when, while, where, as, since, if, although, because*.

There are a few things you might want to know about these clause starters:

- The clause they begin has a subject and a verb (noun and verb).
- It is a dependent clause (sometimes called a subordinate clause), which means it cannot stand alone as a sentence. It depends on another clause (the main clause) to make it legal.

When it starts a clause, write a little *cl* over each www.asia.b word.

To help you remember the list of clause starters (www.asia.b), add the Week 23 grammar card to your collection. Keep the rest of your grammar cards handy for review as you need them.

FIX IT

Read	Read the sentence.
Vocabulary	Look up the bolded word in a dictionary and add the key word definition to your notebook.
Day 1	Your teacher will help you mark and fix the first passage. Complete the rewrite after fixing.
Days 2–4	Use the abbreviations at the top of the next page and the grammar cards to help you remember how to mark the passage. Your teacher will help you with anything you miss. Remember, a mistake is an opportunity to learn. Continue to evaluate the dress-ups used this week. Out of all the choices, circle the single strongest verb, adjective, and -ly adverb.
Rewrite	Copy the corrected passage into a separate notebook.

- Be sure to double-space and indent where indicated.
- Do not copy the markings, just the story.
- Remember to use capital letters properly.
- Carefully copy the punctuation and use end marks.

Page 48, *Fix It! Grammar:* **The Nose Tree, Student Book 1**

DAY 1

    ar   *adj*   *n*   *ly*   *vb*   *ar*   *adj*

the ~~to/~~two~~/too~~ soldiers instantly decided to ~~/two/too~~ follow the **elongated**

  n   *cl* *pr* *vb* *cc* *vb* *pr*   *n*

nose where it led and find its ~~/it's~~ owner.

Fixes

elongated: drawn out to greater length

Indent. Is this a new topic, speaker, place, or time? Answer: No. It continues where last week left off with the soldiers finding the long nose.

Capitalization. Capitalize the first word of a sentence.

Homophones. Have students cross out the incorrect *to/two/too* (twice) and check the spelling when copied. Have students cross out the incorrect *its/it's*, explain the meaning of the correct one, and check the spelling when copied. This should be *its* expressing possession: the owner of the nose, or its owner.

End marks. Period at end of statement.

Grammar Notations

Verbs. *decided, led, find.*

   ✦ **Advanced.** Technically, *find* is not a verb because it is an infinitive with *to* implied in front of it: *to follow* and *to find*. Few students would see this, and many will also mark *follow* as a verb. Let students mark them either as verbs or not since *follow* and *find* are verbals performing an action.

-ly adverbs. *instantly.* Ask: What part of speech does this adverb describe? Answer: the verb *decided*.

Coordinating conjunctions. *and.*

   ✦ **Advanced.** Ask what words this cc joins. Answer: two verbals, *to follow* and *(to) find*. See Verbs above.

Clause starters. *where.* From the parts of speech notations, show that there is a subject (noun or pronoun) and verb after this clause starter (also called a subordinating conjunction): where *it led*.

✎ **Teacher's note.** Although the clause starters are technically called subordinating conjunctions, it is helpful to students to give them simpler terms to start. Giving students a list of common clause starters (*when, while, where, as, since, if, although, because*) makes it even easier.

DAY 2

cl   pr   vb   pr   adj   n   w-w

¶ when they tracked down ~~there~~/their/~~they're~~ **pitiable** comrade, who

vb   vb   adj   prep   ar   n   pr   v

was lying helpless <u>under the apple tree</u>, they groaned.

Fixes

pitiable: miserable; deserving pity

Indent. Is this a new topic, speaker, place, or time? Answer: Yes. Start a new paragraph because of a new place and topic, finding and trying to help the second soldier.

Capitalization. Capitalize the first word of a sentence.

Homophones. Have students cross out the incorrect *there/their/they're* and check the spelling when copied.

End marks. Period at end of statement.

Grammar Notations

Articles and nouns. *comrade, the apple tree.*

> ✧ **Advanced.** *apple* in *apple tree* counts as part of a compound noun, a noun that is formed from two nouns combined.

Verbs. *tracked, was lying, groaned.* Ask: Which of these are helping verbs? Answer: *was,* which helps along *lying.*

Adjectives. *pitiable, helpless.* If students do not recognize that *helpless* is an adjective, since it does not describe a noun immediately after it, let it go.

> ♡ **Grammar lovers.** *Helpless* modifies *who.*

Prepositional phrases. *under the apple tree.* Ask students to show how the phrase fits the pattern: preposition + noun, no verb. They should use the parts of speech notations to show this. Answer: *under ... apple tree.*

> ✧ **Advanced.** You can tell that *down* is an adverb and not a preposition here because "tracked down" makes sense but "down their pitiable comrade" does not.

Clause starters. *when.* From the parts of speech notations, show that there is a subject (noun or pronoun) and verb after this clause starter (also called a subordinating conjunction): When *they tracked.*

***Who-which* clauses.** Mark with *w-w* and read aloud: *who was lying helpless under the apple tree.*

> Ask: What noun immediately before it does this *who* clause describe?
> Answer: *comrade.*

> Ask students to show you where the commas are placed.

✏ **Teacher's note.**
Do not feel as if you need to cover all these points in depth. They are provided for your reference, but if a point is too much for your student, you can let it go.

DAY 3

<u>w</u>hat *ly* exactly *vb* could *pr* they *vb* do to **assist** ~~there~~/their ~~they're~~ *pr* friend *n* since *cl* they *pr*

had *vb* no *adj* long *n* cart *prep* <u>for *pr* his *n* nose</u>?

Fixes

assist: aid; help

Indent. Is this a new topic, speaker, place, or time? Answer: No, because it continues with their trying to help their friend.

Capitalization. Capitalize the first word of a sentence.

Homophones. Have students cross out the incorrect *there/their/they're* and check the spelling when copied.

End marks. Question mark at end of question.

Grammar Notations

Verbs. *could do, had.* Ask: Which of these are helping verbs? Answer: *could*, which helps along *do*.

✧ **Advanced.** *had* is sometimes a helping verb, but not in this sentence because there is no other verb right after it for it to help along.

Prepositional phrases. *for his nose.*

Ask students to use the parts of speech notations to show how the phrase fits the pattern: preposition + noun, no verb. Answer: *for ... nose.*

Clause starters. *since.*

From the parts of speech notations, show that there is a subject (noun or pronoun) and verb after this clause starter (subordinating conjunction): Since *they had.*

DAY 4

ly   *pr*   *vb*   *pr*   *cl*   *pr*   *n*

<u>i</u>mmediately they tried to ~~/two/too~~ carry him but **in vain** because his nose

vb   *adj*

was ~~to/two/~~too lengthy.

Fixes

Indent. Is this a new topic, speaker, place, or time? Answer: No. It continues with their helping their friend.

Capitalization. Capitalize the first word of a sentence.

Homophones. Have students cross out the incorrect *to/two/too* (twice) and check the spelling when copied. Ask students to tell you what *too* means in "too lengthy" (too much; beyond what is desirable).

End marks. Period at end of statement.

Grammar Notations

Verbs. *tried, was.*

> ✧ **Advanced.** If they do not catch *was*, show students a list of *be* verbs (*am, is, are, was, were*), remind them they are all verbs, and ask them to identify the *be* verb in this sentence.

> ✧ **Advanced.** If students mark the infinitive *to carry* as a verb, let them even though it is not technically a verb.

-ly adverbs. *Immediately*. Ask: What part of speech does this adverb describe? Answer: the verb *tried*.

Clause starters. *because*. From the parts of speech notations, show that there is a subject (noun or pronoun) and verb after this clause starter (subordinating conjunction): *because his nose was.*

Style

Have your students choose the single best of the following dress-ups from this week's sentences. Discuss their answers. Best possibilities:

Strong verbs. *tracked down, groaned*. If they choose *assist*, accept that too even though it is a verbal and not technically a verb.

Quality adjectives. *elongated, pitiable.*

-ly adverbs. *instantly, immediately.*

in vain: without effect; to no purpose

In vain is an idiom, which is an expression that does not make literal sense. Do not worry about parts of speech in idioms.

✏ **Teacher's note.** Usually *but* is a coordinating conjunction, but sometimes it acts as other parts of speech. In this sentence, it is an adverb meaning *only* or *just*.

STUDENT REWRITE

Since this passage continues without another indentation, be sure students continue writing where last week's passage left off.

The two soldiers instantly decided to follow the elongated nose where it led and find its owner.

When they tracked down their pitiable comrade, who was lying helpless under the apple tree, they groaned. What exactly could they do to assist their friend since they had no long cart for his nose? Immediately they tried to carry him but in vain because his nose was too lengthy.

Week 24

Review

LEARN IT

There are no new concepts for today. See if you can answer the questions below. If not, check your grammar cards for the answers.

- What is a test for adjectives?
- Can you list the clause starters (subordinating conjunctions)? (Hint: www.asia.b)

Do you remember what these vocabulary words mean? If not, look them up in your vocabulary list in the back of your notebook.

- dwell
- elegant
- roamed
- crafty
- observed

FIX IT

Read   Read the sentence.

Vocabulary   Look up the bolded word in a dictionary and decide which definition best fits the meaning of the word in this sentence. Add the definition to the list in the back of your notebook.

Day 1   Your teacher will help you mark and fix the first passage. Complete the rewrite after fixing.

Days 2–4   Use the abbreviations at the top of the next page and the grammar cards to help you remember how to mark the passage. Your teacher will help you with anything you miss. Remember, a mistake is an opportunity to learn. Continue to evaluate the dress-ups used this week. Out of all the choices, circle the single strongest verb, adjective, and -ly adverb.

Rewrite   Copy the corrected passage into a separate notebook.

- Be sure to double-space and indent where indicated.
- Do not copy the markings, just the story.
- Remember to use capital letters properly.
- Carefully copy the punctuation and use end marks.

Page 50, *Fix It! Grammar:* **The Nose Tree, Student Book 1**

DAY 1

¶ *prep* *n* *pr* *adj* *n* *ar* *n* *prep* *ar* *adj*
before long, ~~there~~/their ~~/they're~~ old **benefactor**, the dwarf with the red

n *vb*
jacket, appeared.

Fixes

Indent. Is this a new topic, speaker, place, or time? Answer: Yes. Start a new paragraph because of a new topic, the arrival of the dwarf.

Capitalization. Capitalize the first word of a sentence.

Homophones. Have students cross out the incorrect *there/their/they're* and check the spelling when copied.

End marks. Period at end of statement.

> **benefactor:** someone who supports or helps someone else, especially by giving money or valuables

Grammar Notations

Verbs. *appeared.* Ask: Who is doing this action? Answer: the dwarf.

Prepositional phrases. *Before long, with the red jacket.*

Ask students to use the parts of speech notations to show how each phrase fits the pattern: preposition + noun, no verb. Remind your students that articles (*the*) and adjectives (*red*) can come between the preposition and noun, just no verbs. Answer: *Before long; with … jacket.*

If students have trouble recognizing that *long* is a noun in this sentence, just point out that it means a comparatively long time. *Long* is usually used as an adjective, but it does not describe a noun here so cannot be an adjective.

DAY 2

¶ "why, ~~what is~~ up, my friend?" he remarked while he softly **chuckled.**

Fixes

chuckled: laughed with amusement

Indent. Is this a new topic, speaker, place, or time? Answer: Yes. Start a new paragraph because of a new speaker.

Quotation. Ask your students to explain why quotation marks are placed where they are. Answer: They enclose the dwarf's speech.

Capitalization. Capitalize the first word of a sentence.

Also, the quotation is followed by a lowercase word (*he*) even though it follows an end mark since "he remarked" sets up the quotation and is part of that same sentence. Check that your student does not capitalize *he*.

Apostrophes. Have students form *what is* into its contraction *what's*. Remind them that contractions work well in speech.

End marks. Check that your students have added a question mark at the end of the quoted sentence. It goes inside the quotation marks since the dwarf is asking a question. Period at end of statement.

Grammar Notations

✏ **Teacher's note.**
What's up is an idiom used as a greeting. It means both "How are you?" and "What is happening?" Tell your students not to worry about identifying parts of speech in idioms.

Pronouns. If your students do not label *my*, explain that it is another possessive pronoun. It is not in their list of pronouns to look for because it occurs infrequently in *Nose Tree*.

-ly adverbs. *softly.* Ask: What part of speech does this adverb describe? Answer: the verb *chuckled.*

Clause starters. *while.* Ask: Can you find a subject (noun or pronoun) and verb after this clause starter? Use your parts of speech notations to locate them. Answer: while *he chuckled.*

DAY 3

cl	ar	n	vb	adj	pr	vb	prep ar	n	pr vb

¶ since the problem was obvious, he continued <u>after a pause</u>, "<u>well</u>, i must

ly	vb	ar	n	prep pr

plainly find an **antidote** <u>for you</u>."

Fixes

Indent. Is this a new topic, speaker, place, or time? Answer: Yes. Start a new paragraph even though it is the same speaker. This helps the reader see that the speaker hesitates a moment before continuing on, so time has passed.

Capitalization. Capitalize the first word of a sentence. Also capitalize the first word of a quoted sentence (*Well*) and capitalize the pronoun *I*.

End marks. Period at end of statement goes inside closing quotations.

Grammar Notations

Verbs. *was, continued, must find*. Ask: Which of these are helping verbs? Answer: *must*, the only verb that has an action verb after it (*find*) that it is helping along.

♡ **Grammar lovers.** *was* is a linking verb, linking the subject (*problem*) to a subject complement (*obvious*) that describes it: the obvious problem.

Adjectives. *obvious*. If your students have trouble recognizing that this is an adjective, let it go. It comes after the noun instead of before it and is not as descriptive as many adjectives are.

Prepositional phrases. *after a pause, for you*. Ask students to use the parts of speech notations to show how each phrase fits the pattern: preposition + noun/pronouns, no verb.

-ly adverbs. *plainly*. Ask: What part of speech does this adverb describe? Answer: the verb *find*.

Clause starters. *Since*. Ask: Can you find a subject (noun or pronoun) and verb after this clause starter? Use your parts of speech notations to locate them. Answer: *problem was*.

antidote: a medicine or other remedy for countering injuries or unwanted effects

✏ **Teacher's note.** Your student does not need to master subject/verb yet. Continue to point it out until it becomes easy.

DAY 4

pr   vb   pr   ar n prep adj   adj   n w-w   vb

¶ he told them to select a pear from another special tree, which **flourished**

nearby.

Fixes

flourished: thrived; grew luxuriantly

Indent. Is this a new topic, speaker, place, or time? Answer: Yes. Start a new paragraph because of a new topic, turning from direct speech (quotation) to indirect speech (something like "he said that … ").

Capitalization. Capitalize the first word of a sentence.

End marks. Period at end of statement.

Grammar Notations

Prepositional phrases. *from another special tree*. Ask students to use the parts of speech notations to show how the phrase fits the pattern: preposition + noun, no verb. Remind them that other parts of speech (but no verbs) can go inside. Answer: *from … tree*. *Another* and *special* are not verbs.

Who-which clauses. Read the entire clause aloud: *which flourished nearby*.

Ask: What noun immediately before it does this *which* clause describe? Answer: tree.

Ask students to show you where the commas are placed (none at end because of the period).

Style

Have your students choose the single best of the following dress-ups from this week's sentences. Discuss their answers. Best possibilities:

Strong verbs. *chuckled, flourished*.

Quality adjectives. *obvious, special*.

-ly adverbs. *softly, plainly*.

STUDENT REWRITE

Before long, their old benefactor, the dwarf with the red jacket, appeared.

"Why, what's up, my friend?" he remarked while he softly chuckled.

Since the problem was obvious, he continued after a pause, "Well, I must plainly find an antidote for you."

He told them to select a pear from another special tree, which flourished nearby.

Week 25

Your and You're

Read the Learn It part with your students.

Adjust the lessons as needed.

This week your students will differentiate between *your* and *you're*.

Grammar Cards. Have your students find the new grammar card to add to their collection.

Once you have read the Learn It part, show your student how to apply it to the Day 1 passage.

LEARN IT

Usage   Be careful with these words that sound the same.

Your is the possessive pronoun (*your* cat, *your* nose, *your* grandpa).

You're is a contraction of the words *you are*. (*You're* welcome!)

To help you remember these things for future lessons, add the Week 25 grammar card to your collection. Keep the remaining cards handy for review.

FIX IT

Read   Read the sentence.

Vocabulary   Look up the bolded word in a dictionary and decide which definition best fits the meaning of the word in this sentence. Add the definition to the list in the back of your notebook.

Day 1   Your teacher will help you mark and fix the first passage. Complete the rewrite after fixing.

Days 2–4   Use the abbreviations at the top of the next page and the grammar cards to help you remember how to mark the passage. Your teacher will help you with anything you miss. Remember, a mistake is an opportunity to learn. Continue to evaluate the dress-ups used this week. Out of all the choices, circle the single strongest verb, adjective, and -ly adverb.

Rewrite   Copy the corrected passage into a separate notebook.

- Be sure to double-space and indent where indicated.
- Do not copy the markings, just the story.
- Remember to use capital letters properly.
- Carefully copy the punctuation and use end marks.

Page 52, *Fix It! Grammar:* **The Nose Tree, Student Book 1**

DAY 1

the soldier's nose

| cl | pr | vb | ar | n | ar | n | prep | ar | n | vb | | vb | prep | pr |

¶ after he ate the pear, ~~the nose of the soldier~~ was soon brought to its,/it's

| adj | n | cc | pr | vb | ar | n | prep | n |

rightful size, and he thanked the dwarf with gratitude.

Fixes

rightful: proper; appropriate; fitting

Indent. Is this a new topic, speaker, place, or time? Answer: Yes. Start a new paragraph because of a new topic, the cure.

Capitalization. Capitalize the first word of a sentence.

Usage. Have students cross out the incorrect *its/it's*, explain the meaning of the correct one, and check the spelling when copied. *Its* expresses possession: the size of the nose, or *its size*.

Apostrophes for ownership. In their rewrite ask students to convert "the nose of the soldier" into a phrase with a possessive apostrophe: *the soldier's nose*. Discuss that the second sounds better because it is not wordy.

End marks. Period at end of statement.

Grammar Notations

Verbs. *ate, was brought, thanked.* Ask: Which of these are helping verbs? Answer: *was,* which helps *brought* along.

Prepositional phrases. *of the soldier* (which disappears in the rewrite), *to its rightful size, with gratitude.*

Ask students to use the parts of speech notations to show how the phrase fits the pattern: preposition + noun, no verb. Remind them that other words (but no verbs) can go in between. Answer: *of … soldier; to … size; with gratitude.*

Coordinating conjunctions. *and.*

✧ **Advanced.** The cc *and* joins two main clauses with a comma before it. This advanced concept will be taught in later *Fix It!* stories.

Clause starters. *After*

✧ **Advanced.** *After* is usually a preposition but sometimes starts a clause. You can tell it is a clause starter (subordinating conjunction) because it is followed by a subject and verb: *he ate.* Because it is usually a preposition, we do not include it in the main www words.

DAY 2

> *I'll*
>
> cl   pr vb   adj   pr vb vb   n   prep pr
> ¶ "because ~~your/~~you're so goodhearted, ~~i will~~ do something more for you,
>
> vb   ar   adj   n
> ~~to/two/~~too ," declared the **genial** dwarf.

Fixes

genial: pleasantly cheerful

Indent. Is this a new topic, speaker, place, or time? Answer: Yes. Start a new paragraph because of a new speaker.

Capitalization. Capitalize the first word of a sentence and the personal pronoun *I*.

Homophones and usage. Have students cross out the incorrect *your/you're* and *to/two/too* and check the spelling when copied. Ask them what this *too* means. Answer: also.

Quotations. Check that students copy the quotation marks correctly. Remind them:

- Quotation marks enclose speech.
- Use a comma (after *too*) when a speaking verb (*declared*) sets up the quotation that comes before or after it.
- Commas and periods go inside closing quotation marks.

Apostrophes. Have students form *I will* into its contraction *I'll*. Remind them that contractions work well in speech.

End marks. Period at end of statement.

Grammar Notations

Verbs. *are* (in *you're*), *will do*, *declared*. Ask: Which of these are helping verbs? Answer: *will*, which helps out *do*.

Prepositional phrases. *for you*. Ask students to use the parts of speech notations to show how the phrase fits the pattern: preposition + noun/pronoun, no verb. Note that pronouns can substitute for nouns in this pattern.

Clause starters. *Because*. Ask: Can you find a subject (noun or pronoun) and verb after this clause starter? Use your parts of speech notations to locate them. Answer: *you're* (you are).

DAY 3

vb prep ar   *n*   *cc*   *vb*   *pr*   *prep*   *adj*   *n*   *pr*

"go to the princess and get her to **feast** on even more apples than you

vb

consumed.

Fixes

feast: to eat with delight

Indent. Is this a new topic, speaker, place, or time? Answer: No indent. Do not start a new paragraph because the dwarf is still speaking on the same topic.

Capitalization. Capitalize the first word of a sentence.

Quotations. Check that students copy the quotation marks correctly.

End marks. Period at end of statement but no close quotations because he is not finished speaking.

Grammar Notations

Verbs. *go, get, consumed*. If students mark the infinitive *to feast* as a verb, accept it.

　✧ **Advanced.** Students may not recognize that *go* and *get* are verbs because their subject, *you*, is hidden (*you* do these things). Explain that in commands, *you* is understood but not stated.

Prepositional phrases. *to the princess, on even more apples*. Ask students to use the parts of speech notations to show how the phrase fits the pattern: preposition + noun/pronoun, no verb. Answer: *to … princess; on … apples*.

Adjectives. *more*. Students may have trouble identifying this adjective. If so, simply point out to them that it describes *apples* (more apples) and that only adjectives can describe nouns.

Coordinating conjunctions. *and*. Ask: What words does this cc join? Answer: two verbs, *go* and *get*.

DAY 4

pr	vb	vb		pr	vb	prep	pr	cl	pr	n	vb	vb	adj

<u>you</u> will **obtain** what you want <u>from her</u> because her nose will grow twenty

n		pr	vb

times as long as yours did."

Fixes

obtain: get

Indent. Is this a new topic, speaker, place, or time? Answer: No, because the dwarf is still speaking on the same topic.

Capitalization. Capitalize the first word of a sentence.

End marks. Period at end of statement inside closing quotations.

Grammar Notations

Articles and nouns. *nose, times.* Students may have trouble seeing that *times* is a noun. You could point out that *twenty* describes it, and *twenty* is an adjective here, which makes *times* a noun.

Pronouns. If your students do not label *yours*, explain that it is another possessive pronoun but not in their list of pronouns to look for because this is its only appearance in *Nose Tree*.

✏ **Teacher's note.** Show that *yours* is possessive, but like the possessive *its*, *yours* does not use an apostrophe to mark ownership. This is true of all possessive pronouns: *its, yours, ours, his, hers, theirs, whose.*

Verbs. *will obtain, want, will grow, did.* Ask: Which of these verbs are helping verbs? Answer: *will*, which helps out *obtain*; and *will*, which helps out *grow*. *Did* is sometimes a helping verb but not in this sentence because it is not followed by an action verb.

Prepositional phrases. *from her.* Ask students to use the parts of speech notations to show how the phrase fits the pattern: preposition + noun/pronoun, no verb.

Clause starters. *because.* (See the Teacher's Note below for *as*.) From the parts of speech notations, show that there is a subject (noun or pronoun) and verb after this clause starter: *because her nose will grow.*

✏ **Teacher's note.** Do not worry about marking *as* in the idiom *as long as*. Students should not worry about parts of speech in idioms.

Style

Have your students choose the single best of the following dress-ups from this week's sentences. Discuss their answers. Best possibilities:

Strong verbs. *declared, consumed, obtain.*

Quality adjectives. *rightful, goodhearted, genial.*

STUDENT REWRITE

After he ate the pear, the soldier's nose was soon brought to its rightful size, and he thanked the dwarf with gratitude.

"Because you're so goodhearted, I'll do something more for you, too," declared the genial dwarf. "Go to the princess and get her to feast on even more apples than you consumed. You will obtain what you want from her because her nose will grow twenty times as long as yours did."

Week 26

Review

LEARN IT

There are no new concepts for today. See if you can answer the questions below. If not, check your grammar cards for the answers.

- What is a pronoun? Can you list a few?

Do you remember what these vocabulary words mean? If not, look them up in your vocabulary list in the back of your notebook.

- rashly
- confided
- cunning
- divulged
- suspected

FIX IT

Read	Read the sentence.
Vocabulary	Look up the bolded word in a dictionary and decide which definition best fits the meaning of the word in this sentence. Add the definition to the list in the back of your notebook.
Day 1	Your teacher will help you mark and fix the first passage. Complete the rewrite after fixing.
Days 2–4	Use the abbreviations at the top of the next page and the grammar cards to help you remember how to mark the passage. Your teacher will help you with anything you miss. Remember, a mistake is an opportunity to learn. Continue to evaluate the dress-ups used this week. Out of all the choices, circle the single strongest verb, adjective, and -ly adverb.
Rewrite	Copy the corrected passage into a separate notebook.

  - Be sure to double-space and indent where indicated.
  - Do not copy the markings, just the story.
  - Remember to use capital letters properly.
  - Carefully copy the punctuation and use end marks.

Page 54, *Fix It! Grammar:* The Nose Tree, Student Book 1

DAY 1

      cl   pr   vb   pr   vb   pr   adj   n   ly

¶ when he finished, they thanked ~~there~~/their/~~they're~~ old friend **heartily**

prep adj pr   n
for all his kindness.

Fixes

heartily: warmly; affectionately; with heartfelt sincerity

Indent. Is this a new topic, speaker, place, or time? Answer: Yes. Start a new paragraph because of a new topic, pulling out of a speech and turning to the soldiers' reaction.

Capitalization. Capitalize the first word of a sentence.

Homophones. Have students cross out the incorrect *there/their/they're* and check the spelling when copied.

End marks. Period at end of statement.

Grammar Notations

Adjectives. *old, all.* If students are confused, explain that *all* describes *kindness*, and only adjectives can describe nouns.

Prepositional phrases. *for all his kindness.* Ask students to use the parts of speech notations to show how the phrase fits the pattern: preposition + noun/pronoun, no verb. Answer: *for ... kindness.*

Clause starters. *When.* From the parts of speech notations, show that there is a subject (noun or pronoun) and verb after this clause starter (subordinating conjunction): When *he finished.*

DAY 2

pr vb vb   ar adj n w-w vb   vb prep ar n

<u>it</u> was agreed that the poor soldier who had already suffered <u>from the power</u>

prep ar n vb vb ar n

<u>of the apple</u> should **undertake** the task**.**

Fixes

undertake: take upon oneself

Indent. Is this a new topic, speaker, place, or time? Answer: No. The passage continues to talk about their plans.

Capitalization. Capitalize the first word of a sentence.

End marks. Period at end of statement.

Grammar Notations

Pronouns. *it.*

> 💚 **Grammar lovers.** Here, *it* refers to a concept about to be mentioned instead of a noun before it.

Verbs. *was agreed, had suffered, should undertake.* Ask: Which of these are helping verbs? Answer: *was* (helps *agreed*), *had* (helps *suffered*), *should* (helps *undertake*).

Prepositional phrases. *from the power, of the apple.* Ask students to use the parts of speech notations to show how the phrase fits the pattern: preposition + noun/pronoun, no verb. Answer: *from … power; of … apple.*

Who-which clauses. Read the entire clause aloud: *who had already suffered from the power of the apple.* Ask: What noun immediately before it does this *who* clause describe? Answer: *soldier.*

> ✧ **Advanced.** No commas because this *who* clause is needed in the sentence to identify which of the three soldiers is meant.

> 💚 **Grammar lovers.** Most *who-which* clauses are nonessential (take commas), but if they change the meaning of the sentence if removed, they are essential and do not take commas. See Grammar Glossary: Punctuation: Commas: Rule 15: Essential-Nonessential Elements, page G-24. This is advanced even for middle school students.

DAY 3

a gardener's son

ar   adj   n   pr   vb   pr   prep ar n prep ar   n   cc   vb   prep

¶ the next day, he **costumed** himself as ~~a son of a gardener~~ and hurried to

ar   n   prep ar   n

~~the palace of~~ the king's *palace.*

Fixes

costumed: to dress in a costume

Indent. Is this a new topic, speaker, place, or time? Answer: Yes. Start a new paragraph because of a new time.

Capitalization. Capitalize the first word of a sentence.

Apostrophes for ownership. In their rewrite ask students to convert "a son of a gardener" *and* "the palace of the king" into phrases with a possessive apostrophe. Answer: *a gardener's son; the king's palace.*

End marks. Period at end of statement.

Grammar Notations

Pronouns. If students labeled the reflexive pronoun *himself,* praise them! If not, just explain that it is another kind of pronoun.

Prepositional phrases. *as a son, of a gardener* (becomes *as a gardener's son*), *to the palace, of the king* (becomes *to the king's palace*).

Ask students to use the parts of speech notations to show how each phrase fits the pattern: preposition + noun/pronoun, no verb. Answer: *as … son; of … gardener; to … palace; of … king.*

✧ **Advanced.** If students ask about *as,* which usually starts a clause, point out that it is sometimes a preposition. It is a clause starter when there is a subject and verb after it; it is a preposition when it is followed by a noun with no verb, as here: *as a gardener's son.*

Coordinating conjunctions. *and.* Ask: What words does this cc join? Answer: two verbs, *costumed* and *hurried.*

DAY 4

$\underset{he}{\text{pr}}$ boldly declared he had apples to sell, so **exquisite** and juicy that they had

pr   ly   vb   pr vb   n   adj   cc   adj   pr   vb

vb   vb
never been enjoyed there ~~/their/they're~~ before.

Fixes

exquisite: of rare excellence

Indent. Is this a new topic, speaker, place, or time? Answer: No. This continues the soldier's plot to retrieve their treasures.

Capitalization. Capitalize the first word of a sentence.

Homophones. Have students cross out the incorrect *there/their/they're* and check the spelling when copied. This one is *there* meaning in that place.

End marks. Period at end of statement.

Grammar Notations

Verbs. *declared, had, had been enjoyed.* Ask: Which of these are helping verbs? Answer: *had been,* which help out *enjoyed.*

> If students are puzzled why the first *had* is not a helping verb when the second one is, point out that the first is not followed by another verb to help along.

-ly adverbs. *boldly.* Ask: What part of speech does this adverb describe? Answer: the verb *declared.*

Coordinating conjunctions. *and.* Ask: What words does this cc join? Answer: two adjectives, *exquisite* and *juicy.*

Style

Have your students choose the single best of the following dress-ups from this week's sentences. Discuss their answers. Best possibilities:

Strong verbs. *undertake, costumed, hurried.*

Quality adjectives. *exquisite, juicy.*

-ly adverbs. *heartily, boldly.*

STUDENT REWRITE

When he finished, they thanked their old friend heartily for all his kindness. It was agreed that the poor soldier who had already suffered from the power of the apple should undertake the task.

The next day, he costumed himself as a gardener's son and hurried to the king's palace. He boldly declared he had apples to sell, so exquisite and juicy that they had never been enjoyed there before.

Week 27

Review

LEARN IT

There are no new concepts for today. See if you can answer the questions below. If not, check your grammar cards for the answers.

- Can you name a few helping verbs?

Do you remember what these vocabulary words mean? If not, look them up in your vocabulary list in the back of your notebook.

- lingered
- ordinarily
- covetous
- despair
- immense

FIX IT

Read	Read the sentence.
Vocabulary	Look up the bolded word in a dictionary and decide which definition best fits the meaning of the word in this sentence. Add the definition to the list in the back of your notebook.
Day 1	Your teacher will help you mark and fix the first passage. Complete the rewrite after fixing.
Days 2–4	Use the abbreviations at the top of the next page and the grammar cards to help you remember how to mark the passage. Your teacher will help you with anything you miss. Remember, a mistake is an opportunity to learn. Continue to evaluate the dress-ups used this week. Out of all the choices, circle the single strongest verb, adjective, and -ly adverb.
Rewrite	Copy the corrected passage into a separate notebook.

- Be sure to double-space and indent where indicated.
- Do not copy the markings, just the story.
- Remember to use capital letters properly.
- Carefully copy the punctuation and use end marks.

Page 56, *Fix It! Grammar:* The Nose Tree, Student Book 1

DAY 1

	ar	n	vb	pr	n			ar	adj	cc	adj	n

¶ the princess **appointed** her maid to buy all the ripe and rosy apples.

Fixes

appointed: to assign to a task

Indent. Is this a new topic, speaker, place, or time? Answer: Yes. Start a new paragraph because of a new topic, the princess's response.

Capitalization. Capitalize the first word of a sentence.

End marks. Period at end of statement.

Grammar Notations

Verbs. *appointed.* If your student marks the infinitive *to buy* as a verb, accept it.

Adjectives. *ripe, rosy.*

✧ **Advanced.** *All* is a third adjective, along with *ripe* and *rosy*, but not one students will likely catch and too advanced to teach now.

Coordinating conjunctions. *and.* Ask: What words does this cc join? Answer: two adjectives, *ripe* and *rosy*.

DAY 2

    ar   n   ly   vb   ar   n   cl   pr   vb

<u>t</u>he princess greedily **gobbled** a dozen before she ~~to / two /~~ too began

                        vb   pr   n

to ~~/ two / too~~ wonder what ailed her nose.

Fixes

> **gobbled:** swallowed hastily in large pieces

Indent. Is this a new topic, speaker, place, or time? Answer: No. The sentence continues to focus on her eating the apples.

Capitalization. Capitalize the first word of a sentence.

Homophones. Have students cross out the incorrect *to/two/too* (twice) and check the spelling when copied.

> Ask students to explain the meaning of each. Answer: The first *too* means *also*; the second is the preposition *to* in the infinitive *to wonder*.

> ♡ **Grammar lovers.** Infinitives are verbals formed by placing *to* in front of the simple present form of a verb (like *to sneeze*). Infinitives function as adjectives, adverbs, and nouns but never as verbs. Students do not have to understand infinitives yet.

End marks. Period at end of statement.

Grammar Notations

Verbs. *gobbled, began, ailed.*

> ✧ **Advanced.** If students want to count the infinitive *to wonder* as a verb, accept it even though infinitives do not function as verbs.

-ly adverbs. *greedily.* Ask: What part of speech does this adverb describe? Answer: the verb *gobbled.*

Clause starters. *before* (advanced only)

> ✧ **Advanced.** Like *after, before* is a clause starter (subordinating conjunction) when it is followed by a subject and verb (before *she began*). Because it is usually a preposition, we do not include it in the main www words.

DAY 3

pr   vb   cc   vb   prep   ar   n   prep ar   n   cc prep ar

it grew and grew down to ~~two~~ ~~too~~ the floor, out the window, and over the

adj   n

spacious garden, ~~to~~ ~~two~~ too.

Fixes

spacious: of a great extent or area; vast

Indent. Is this a new topic, speaker, place, or time? Answer: No, because it continues with her eating of the apples.

Capitalization. Capitalize the first word of a sentence.

Homophones. Have students cross out the incorrect *to/two/too* (twice) and check the spelling when copied. Ask them to tell you what these mean. Answer: The first is the preposition *to*; the second is *too* meaning *also*.

End marks. Period at end of statement.

Grammar Notations

Prepositional phrases. *to the floor, out the window, over the spacious garden.* Ask students to use the parts of speech notations to show how each phrase fits the pattern: preposition + noun/pronoun, no verb: *to … floor; out … window; over … garden.*

  ✧ **Advanced.** *down* is an adverb in this sentence, not a preposition.

Coordinating conjunctions. *and, and.*

  Ask: What words do these cc's join? Answer: The first *and* joins two verbs, *grew* and *grew*.

  ✧ **Advanced.** The second *and* joins three prepositional phrases. Point out that when we have a series of three or more of the same item, commas separate them.

DAY 4

	cl	pr	vb	ar	n	ar	n	ly	vb	ar	n

¶ <u>w</u>hen he heard the news, the king hastily sent out a proclamation to

	vb	vb	pr	prep	adj	adj	n

reward whoever would heal her <u>of this **appalling** disease</u>.

Fixes

appalling: causing horror or dismay

Indent. Is this a new topic, speaker, place, or time? Answer: Yes. Start a new paragraph because of a new topic, the initial attempts to help her.

Capitalization. Capitalize the first word of a sentence.

End marks. Period at end of statement.

Grammar Notations

Verbs. *heard, sent, would heal.* Ask: Which of these are helping verbs? Answer: *would*, which helps along *heal*.

   ✧ **Advanced.** If students label *out a proclamation* as a prepositional phrase, it is fine, but *out* is actually an adverb going with *sent* to mean issued or dispatched.

Adjectives. *this, appalling.*

   ✧ **Advanced.** Students may miss the adjective *this*. Just point out that it describes the noun *disease* (*this disease*) so must be an adjective.

-ly adverbs. *hastily.* Ask: What part of speech does this adverb describe? Answer: the verb *sent out*.

Prepositional phrases. *of this appalling disease.* Ask students to use the parts of speech notations to show how each phrase fits the pattern: preposition + noun/pronoun, no verb: *of … disease.*

Clause starters. *When.* From the parts of speech notations, show that there is a subject (noun or pronoun) and verb after this clause starter (subordinating conjunction): *When he heard.*

Style

Have your students choose the single best of the following dress-ups from this week's sentences. Discuss their answers. Best possibilities:

Strong verbs. *appointed, gobbled, ailed.*

Quality adjectives. *ripe, rosy, spacious, appalling.*

-ly adverbs. *greedily, hastily.*

STUDENT REWRITE

The princess appointed her maid to buy all the ripe and rosy apples. The princess greedily gobbled a dozen before she too began to wonder what ailed her nose. It grew and grew down to the floor, out the window, and over the spacious garden, too.

When he heard the news, the king hastily sent out a proclamation to reward whoever would heal her of this appalling disease.

Week 28

Review

LEARN IT

There are no new concepts for today. See if you can answer the question below. If not, check your grammar cards for the answers.

- What are two ways to use apostrophes?

Do you remember what these vocabulary words mean? If not, look them up in your vocabulary list in the back of your notebook.

- crept
- invaluable
- mournfully
- drifted
- laden

FIX IT

Read	Read the sentence.
Vocabulary	Look up the bolded word in a dictionary and decide which definition best fits the meaning of the word in this sentence. Add the definition to the list in the back of your notebook.
Day 1	Your teacher will help you mark and fix the first passage. Complete the rewrite after fixing.
Days 2–4	Use the abbreviations at the top of the next page and the grammar cards to help you remember how to mark the passage. Your teacher will help you with anything you miss. Remember, a mistake is an opportunity to learn. Continue to evaluate the dress-ups used this week. Out of all the choices, circle the single strongest verb, adjective, and -ly adverb.
Rewrite	Copy the corrected passage into a separate notebook. On Day 4 the thoughts of the soldier are marked with quotation marks.

- Be sure to double-space and indent where indicated.
- Do not copy the markings, just the story.
- Remember to use capital letters properly.
- Carefully copy the punctuation and use end marks.
- Underline thoughts.

Page 58, *Fix It! Grammar:* The Nose Tree, Student Book 1

DAY 1

    cl   *n*   *vb*   *pr*   *n*   *ar*   *n*   *vb* *adj* *n*

although many tried to **alleviate** her suffering, the princess received no relief.

Fixes

alleviate: to lessen or make easier to endure

Indent. Is this a new topic, speaker, place, or time? Answer: No. It picks up where we left off last week about trying to find a remedy.

Capitalization. Capitalize the first word of a sentence.

Spelling. For *receive*, an often misspelled word, remind students of the rule "*i* before *e* except after *c*." This *ie/ei* pair comes after *c* so must be *ei*: *receive*.

End marks. Period at end of statement.

Grammar Notations

Articles and nouns. *many, suffering, the princess, relief.*

> If your student does not mark the noun *many*, explain that often it is an adjective (e.g., *many apples*), but when it is not followed by a noun, as here, it can be a noun in its own right.

Verbs. *tried, received.* If students mark the infinitive *to alleviate* as a verb, accept it.

Clause starters. *Although.* From the parts of speech notations, show that there is a subject (noun or pronoun) and verb after this clause starter (subordinating conjunction): *Although many tried.*

DAY 2

prep ar n   ar adj   n   vb   pr   ly   prep ar   n

¶ <u>after a time</u>, the old soldier clothed himself quite **sprucely** <u>as a doctor.</u>

Fixes

Indent. Is this a new topic, speaker, place, or time? Answer: Yes. Start a new paragraph because of a new time and topic.

Capitalization. Capitalize the first word of a sentence.

End marks. Period at end of statement.

sprucely: neatly; smart in appearance or dress

Grammar Notations

Prepositional phrases. *After a time, as a doctor.* Ask students to use the parts of speech notations to show how each phrase fits the pattern: preposition + noun/pronoun, no verb: *after … time; as … doctor.*

 Advanced. Many students will be confused about *as.* It is one of the www words and is usually a clause starter (subordinating conjunction). However, when there is no subject + verb after it but only a noun, as here, it is a preposition.

Pronouns. If students labeled the reflexive pronoun *himself,* praise them! If not, just explain that it is another kind of pronoun.

-ly adverbs. *sprucely.* Ask: What part of speech does this adverb describe? Answer: the verb *clothed.* If students miss this one, just point out that adverbs sometimes go after the verb they describe.

Institute for Excellence in Writing

DAY 3

<pre>
 pr   vb   pr   vb   ly   vb   pr   cl   pr vb   adj   n
</pre>
h̲e announced he could perfectly **restore** her since he had special skill.

Fixes

restore: to bring back to a normal condition

Indent. Is this a new topic, speaker, place, or time? Answer: No, because it is the same topic about the soldier's posing as a doctor.

Capitalization. Capitalize the first word of a sentence.

End marks. Period at end of statement.

Grammar Notations

Verbs. *announced, could restore, had.*

Ask: Which of these are helping verbs? Answer: *could*, which helps out *restore.*

If students ask, point out that *had* sometimes is a helping verb but only when it is followed by an action verb, which is not the case with *had special skill.*

-ly adverbs. *perfectly.* Ask: What part of speech does this adverb describe? Answer: the verb *restore.*

Clause starters. *since.* From the parts of speech notations, show that there is a subject (noun or pronoun) and verb after the clause starter: since *he had.*

DAY 4

pr vb   n   pr vb   vb   ar n   vb   ar adj   n

¶ "first, ~~its~~/it's time she was **humbled** a little," thought the wise soldier

ly
sensibly.

Fixes

Indent. Is this a new topic, speaker, place, or time? Answer: Yes. Start a new paragraph because of a new speaker. Teach that thoughts count like speech for paragraphing.

> ✏ **Teacher's note.** It is more common to place thoughts in italics than in quotation marks, but because italics are difficult to do in handwriting, students should put thoughts in quotation marks instead.

Capitalization. Capitalize the first word of a sentence.

Usage. Have students cross out the incorrect *its/it's*, explain the meaning of the correct one, and check the spelling when copied. This should be *it's* for the contraction: *it is* time, or *it's* time.

End marks. Period at end of statement.

Grammar Notations

Articles and nouns. *time, a little, the soldier.* Students may have trouble identifying *little* as a noun since it is usually an adjective. Remind them that articles (such as *a*) always point to a noun.

Verbs. *is* (in *it's*), *was humbled, thought.* Ask: Which of these are helping verbs? Answer: *was*, which helps out *humbled*.

> ✦ **Advanced.** The word *is* is not a helping verb here because it is not followed by an action verb.

> ♡ **Grammar lovers.** It is hard to tell whether -ed words following *be* verbs are subject complements or past participles of the verb. The easiest test: If the verb is in passive voice, as here (*was humbled by the soldier*), it is a verb. If it is not in passive voice, the -ed word is likely a subject complement. See Grammar Glossary: Parts of Speech: Adjectives, page G-10, and Additional Rules and Concepts: Passive versus Active Voice, page G-33.

-ly adverbs. *sensibly.* Ask: What part of speech does this adverb describe? Answer: the verb *thought*, which comes before the adverb in this sentence.

Style

Have your students choose the single best of the following dress-ups from this week's sentences. Discuss their answers. Best possibilities:

Strong verbs. *clothed, announced, restore, humbled.*

Quality adjectives. *special.*

-ly adverbs. *sprucely, sensibly.*

---

humbled: lowered in condition, power, or importance

Check that students understand **sensibly**, showing good sense. The soldier realizes she will not give up what she stole easily. Plus, he knows she deserves some punishment.

STUDENT REWRITE

Since this passage continues without another indentation, be sure students continue writing where last week's passage left off.

Although many tried to alleviate her suffering, the princess received no relief.

After a time, the old soldier clothed himself quite sprucely as a doctor.

He announced he could perfectly restore her since he had special skill.

"First, it's time she was humbled a little," thought the wise soldier sensibly.

Week 29

Read the Learn It part with your students.

Adjust the lessons as needed.

This week your students will learn **comparative adjectives**.

Grammar Cards. Have your students find the new grammar card to add to their collection.

Once you have read the Learn It part, show your student how to apply it to the Day 1 passage.

Comparative Adjectives

LEARN IT

Adjectives (adj)
As we learned before, adjectives are descriptive words that describe (or modify) nouns and pronouns. Usually they come before the noun they are describing (the *useful* pen), but they can come after a linking verb (it is *useful*).

Some kinds of adjectives help us evaluate a thing.

- Comparative adjectives are used when comparing just two things. Someone can be *better, smaller, bigger,* or *worse* than someone else.
- Superlative adjectives show the most of three or more things. Someone in a group can be the *best, smallest, biggest,* or *worst.*

The important thing to remember is that the form you use depends on how many things are being compared. If just two, use the *-er* form. If three or more, use the *-est* form. Unfortunately, some of these kinds of adjectives do not end in *-er* or *-est*, so you might want to start collecting them as you find them.

These words still follow the adjectives test (the ____ pen). Just be sure you know how many pens you were choosing from.

To help you remember these things for future lessons, add the Week 29 grammar card to your collection. Keep the remaining cards handy for review.

FIX IT

Read
Read the sentence.

Vocabulary
Look up the bolded word in a dictionary and decide which definition best fits the meaning of the word in this sentence. Add the definition to the list in the back of your notebook.

Day 1
Your teacher will help you mark and fix the first passage. Complete the rewrite after fixing.

Days 2–4
Use the abbreviations at the top of the next page and the grammar cards to help you remember how to mark the passage. Your teacher will help you with anything you miss. Remember, a mistake is an opportunity to learn. Continue to evaluate the dress-ups used this week. Out of all the choices, circle the single strongest verb, adjective, and -ly adverb.

Rewrite
Copy the corrected passage into a separate notebook.

- Be sure to double-space and indent where indicated.
- Do not copy the markings, just the story.
- Remember to use capital letters properly.
- Carefully copy the punctuation and use end marks.

Page 60, *Fix It! Grammar:* The Nose Tree, Student Book 1

DAY 1

	cl	pr	vb	pr	n	ar	n	vb	adj	n	cc

<u>w</u>hile he maintained his disguise, the soldier chopped up some apple and

vb	pr	ar	n

handed her a **dose.**

Fixes

dose: a quantity of medicine

Indent. Is this a new topic, speaker, place, or time? Answer: Arguably a new paragraph, but again, it is short enough and related to his thoughts enough to stay in the same paragraph.

Capitalization. Capitalize the first word of a sentence.

End marks. Period at end of statement.

Grammar Notations

Verbs. *maintained, chopped, handed.*

Ask: How many verb actions does the noun *soldier* perform? Answer: two, *chopped up* and *handed. Maintained* goes with the pronoun *he.*

✧ **Advanced.** If students mark *up some apple* as a prepositional phrase, it is fine. You do not need to teach this, but you could ask: Does "up some apple" make sense? No, because *up* is an adverb going with the verb instead: *chopped up.* Prepositional phrases should make sense by themselves.

Coordinating conjunctions. *and.*

✧ **Advanced.** Ask what words the cc *and* joins. Answer: two verbs, *chopped up* and *handed.*

Clause starters. *While.* From the parts of speech notations, show that there is a subject (noun or pronoun) and verb after this clause starter: While *he maintained.*

DAY 2

cl   ar   n   vb   vb   ar   adj   n   pr   n   vb   adj

¶ <u>as</u> the soldier had **anticipated**, the next day her nose was no better,

w-w   vb   ar   adj   n   prep ar   adj   n

which left the unhappy princess <u>in a dreadful fright</u>.

Fixes

Indent. Is this a new topic, speaker, place, or time? Answer: Yes. Start a new paragraph because of a new time.

Capitalization. Capitalize the first word of a sentence.

End marks. Period at end of statement.

anticipated:
expected; knew would happen

Grammar Notations

Verbs. *had anticipated, was, left.* Ask: Which of these are helping verbs? Answer: *had,* which helps along *anticipated.*

✧ **Advanced.** The verb *was* does not have a verb after it so is not a helping verb here.

Adjectives. *next, better, unhappy, dreadful.*

✐ **Teacher's note.** Students may not recognize that *better* is an adjective describing the noun *nose.*

If your students are ready, explain that it is the comparative form of the adjective *good.* Comparative adjectives end with *-er* and imply a comparison to something else. This sentence compares her nose the next day to her nose the day before, saying it was no better.

Prepositional phrases. *in a dreadful fright.* Ask students to use the parts of speech notations to show how the phrase fits the pattern: preposition + noun/pronoun, no verb: *in … fright.*

Clause starters. *As.* From the parts of speech notations, show that there is a subject (noun or pronoun) and verb after this clause starter: As the *soldier had anticipated.*

***Who-which* clauses.** Read the entire clause aloud: *which left the unhappy princess in a dreadful fright.* Ask students to show you where the commas are placed (none at end).

✐ **Teacher's note.** This *which* clause does not follow a noun it describes, as is usually the case, but modifies the entire idea that comes before it: the fact that her nose was no better. If your students are writing *which* clauses in their papers, at this level *which* should come immediately after the noun it describes. Students often run into difficulty when they try to make their *which* modify an idea instead of a noun.

DAY 3

ar   n   vb   ar   adj   n   prep ar   n   w-w   pr

the doctor then chopped up a **modest** portion <u>of the pear</u>, which he

vb   prep pr

presented <u>to her</u>.

Fixes

modest: limited in amount

Indent. Is this a new topic, speaker, place, or time? Answer: No. It continues to talk about what happened the second day.

Capitalization. Capitalize the first word of a sentence.

End marks. Period at end of statement.

Grammar Notations

Verbs. *chopped, presented.*

Prepositional phrases. *of the pear, to her.* Ask students to use the parts of speech notations to show how each phrase fits the pattern: preposition + noun/pronoun, no verb: *of … pear, to her.*

 Advanced. Some students are confused by what look like prepositions after a verb but without the usual noun afterward. In this case, these words do not function as prepositions but as adverbs that go with that verb. Examples: the soldiers *set out,* the doctor *chopped up.*

Who-which clauses. Read the entire clause aloud: *which he presented to her.*

Ask: What noun immediately before it does this *which* clause describe? Answer: *portion.* If they say *pear,* that is fine!

Ask students to show you where the commas are placed (none at end).

DAY 4

ar   *adj*   *n*   *pr*   *n*   *vb*   *adj*   *cc*   *pr*   *vb*   *adj*   *cl*

¶ the next day her nose was indeed smaller, yet it was bigger than when

ar   *n*   *ly*   *vb*   *prep*   *pr*

the doctor originally began to **meddle** <u>with it</u>.

Fixes

Indent. Is this a new topic, speaker, place, or time? Answer: Yes. Start a new paragraph because of a new time.

Capitalization. Capitalize the first word of a sentence.

End marks. Period at end of statement.

meddle: to involve oneself in a matter without invitation or right

Grammar Notations

Verbs. *was, was, began.* Note: None of these is a helping verb.

Adjectives. *next, smaller, bigger.* If your students missed *smaller* and *bigger*, ask: Do you see any more comparative adjectives here? What are they? Answer: *smaller, bigger.*

-ly adverbs. *originally.* Ask: What part of speech does this adverb describe? Answer: the verb *began.*

Prepositional phrases. *with it.* Ask students to use the parts of speech notations to show how the phrase fits the pattern: preposition + noun/pronoun, no verb.

Coordinating conjunctions. *yet.*

> ✦ **Advanced.** Ask what words this cc joins. Answer: two main clauses. Main clauses have a subject and verb and can stand alone as a sentence.

Clause starters. *when.* From the parts of speech notations, show that there is a subject (noun or pronoun) and verb after this clause starter: when the *doctor* originally *began.*

Style

Have your students choose the single best of the following dress-ups from this week's sentences. Discuss their answers. Best possibilities:

Strong verbs. *maintained, chopped up, handed, had anticipated, presented.*

Quality adjectives. *dreadful, modest.*

-ly adverbs. *originally.*

STUDENT REWRITE

Since this passage continues without another indentation, be sure students continue writing where last week's passage left off.

While he maintained his disguise, the soldier chopped up some apple and handed her a dose.

As the soldier had anticipated, the next day her nose was no better, which left the unhappy princess in a dreadful fright. The doctor then chopped up a modest portion of the pear, which he presented to her.

The next day her nose was indeed smaller, yet it was bigger than when the doctor originally began to meddle with it.

Week 30

Discuss the Learn
It part with your
students.

Adjust the lessons as
needed.

This week is a review
week.

Review

LEARN IT

There are no new concepts for today. See if you can answer the questions below. If not, check your grammar cards for the answers.

- Finish this sentence: A prepositional phrase has a preposition and a noun but no _____.
- Can you list a few prepositions?

Do you remember what these vocabulary words mean? If not, look them up in your vocabulary list in the back of your notebook.

- peculiar
- forlorn
- detected
- cease
- arched

Be very careful with quotation marks! Notice that in the last passage, the soldier has more to say, so do not close the quotation.

FIX IT

Read	Read the sentence.
Vocabulary	Look up the bolded word in a dictionary and decide which definition best fits the meaning of the word in this sentence. Add the definition to the list in the back of your notebook.
Day 1	Your teacher will help you mark and fix the first passage. Complete the rewrite after fixing.
Days 2–4	Use the abbreviations at the top of the next page and the grammar cards to help you remember how to mark the passage. Your teacher will help you with anything you miss. Remember, a mistake is an opportunity to learn. Continue to evaluate the dress-ups used this week. Out of all the choices, circle the single strongest verb, adjective, and -ly adverb.
Rewrite	Copy the corrected passage into a separate notebook.

- Be sure to double-space and indent where indicated.
- Do not copy the markings, just the story.
- Remember to use capital letters properly.
- Carefully copy the punctuation and use end marks.
- Underline thoughts.

Page 62, *Fix It! Grammar:* **The Nose Tree, Student Book 1**

DAY 1

$$\text{the soldier rightly }\mathbf{judged},\text{ ``i must frighten this cunning princess a little}$$

| ar | n | ly | vb | pr | vb | vb | adj | adj | n | ar | adj |

¶ the soldier rightly **judged**, "i must frighten this cunning princess a little

I'm
more if ~~i am~~ to get what i want <u>from her</u>."

| n | | cl | pr | vb | | pr | vb | prep | pr |

Fixes

Indent. Is this a new topic, speaker, place, or time? Answer: Yes. Start a new paragraph because of a new speaker.

Capitalization. Capitalize the first word of a sentence. Also capitalize the personal pronoun *I* three times.

Quotation marks. We know he is not speaking to anyone, so it is the soldier's thoughts, which we write with quotation marks. Remember: It is more common to place thoughts in italics than in quotation marks, but because italics are difficult to do in handwriting, students should put thoughts in quotation marks instead.

Apostrophes. In their rewrite, have students form *I am* into its contraction *I'm*. Remind them that contractions work well in stories, especially in dialogue, but usually not in formal papers.

End marks. Period at end of statement inside closing quotations.

> **judged:** determined from the circumstances; formed an opinion. Note that *judge* is not a legal term here but used more broadly to refer to someone's thought-out deduction.

Grammar Notations

Articles and nouns. *the soldier, princess, a more.* Students may have trouble recognizing *more* as a noun. Just point out that there is an article before it.

Verbs. *judged, must frighten, am* (in *I'm*), *want.* Ask: Which of these are helping verbs? Answer: *must,* helping out *frighten.*

-ly adverbs. *rightly.* Ask: What part of speech does this adverb describe? Answer: the verb *judged.*

Prepositional phrases. *from her.* Ask students to use the parts of speech notations to show how the phrase fits the pattern: preposition + noun/pronoun, no verb.

Clause starters. *if.* From the parts of speech notations, show that there is a subject (noun or pronoun) and verb after this clause starter (subordinating conjunction): if *I am.*

DAY 2

pr	vb	pr	prep	adj	adj	n	prep ar	n	cc	vb	pr

¶ thus, he left her <u>with another large dose</u> <u>of the apple</u> and indicated he

vb	vb prep ar	n

would call <u>on the **morrow.**</u>

Fixes

Indent. Is this a new topic, speaker, place, or time? Answer: Yes. We are pulling out of his thoughts and into his actions, so it is a new topic.

Capitalization. Capitalize the first word of a sentence.

End marks. Period at end of statement.

Grammar Notations

Verbs. *left, indicated, would call.* Ask: Which of these are helping verbs?
Answer: *would,* which helps along *call.*

> Ask: What noun or pronoun is the subject of *indicated*? Answer: the first *he.* Point out that he is doing two actions, *left* and *indicated.*

Prepositional phrases. *with another large dose, of the apple, on the morrow.*

> Ask students to use the parts of speech notations to show how the phrase fits the pattern: preposition + noun/pronoun, no verb. Answer: *with … dose; of … apple; on … morrow.* Show students that these phrases do not have verbs in them.

Coordinating conjunctions. *and.*

> ✧ **Advanced.** Ask what words the cc *and* joins. Answer: two verbs, *left* and *indicated.*

morrow: the next day

Check that students understand the meaning of **thus**: as a result; consequently.

DAY 3

the princess's enlarged nose

| ar | adj | n | ar | adj | n | prep | ar | n | vb | adj |

¶ <u>t</u>he next day ~~the enlarged nose of the princess~~ was worse than before.

Fixes

enlarged: expanded; grown larger

Indent. Is this a new topic, speaker, place, or time? Answer: Yes. Start a new paragraph because of a new time.

Capitalization. Capitalize the first word of a sentence.

Apostrophes for ownership. In their rewrite ask students to convert "the enlarged nose of the princess" into a phrase with a possessive apostrophe: *the princess's enlarged nose.*

End marks. Period at end of statement.

Grammar Notations

Verbs. *was.*

♡ **Grammar lovers.** *was* is not a helping verb but a linking verb, linking the subject *nose* to the subject complement *worse.*

Adjectives. *next, enlarged, worse.*

✧ **Advanced.** Many students will not recognize that *worse* is an adjective. Mention that it describes the noun *nose* and is the comparative form of the adjective *bad,* expressing the "more bad" of two. A few comparative adjectives do not end in *-er* but have an irregular spelling.

Prepositional phrases. *of the princess* (which disappears in the rewrite). Ask students to use the parts of speech notations to show how the phrase fits the pattern: preposition + noun/pronoun, no verb. Answer: *of … princess.*

DAY 4

pr   *adj*   *n*   *vb*   *ar*   *n*   *n*   *vb*

¶   "my noble lady," pressed the doctor, "something works ~~to/two/~~too

ly   *prep*   *pr*   *n*

heavily against my **remedy.**

Fixes

Indent. Is this a new topic, speaker, place, or time? Answer: Yes. Start a new paragraph because of a new speaker.

Capitalization. Capitalize the first word of a sentence.

Homophones. Have students cross out the incorrect *to/two/too* and check the spelling when copied. Ask them to tell you what *too* means in this sentence. Answer: *too much; to an excessive degree.*

Quotation. Ask: Did you include his words inside quotation marks but not the narrative that interrupts his speech (*pressed the doctor*)? Teach that commas set off narrative interruptions and show that *something* is lowercase because it is in the middle of his sentence. Capitalize the start of a quotation only when it begins a quoted sentence.

Next week, students will continue writing more of his words after *remedy* and should not end with quotation marks until he finishes talking.

End marks. Period at end of statement.

Grammar Notations

Pronouns. If your students do not label *my*, explain that it is another possessive pronoun. It is not in their list of pronouns to look for because it occurs infrequently in *Nose Tree*.

-ly adverbs. *heavily*. Ask: What part of speech does this adverb describe? Answer: the verb *works*.

Prepositional phrases. *against my remedy*. Ask students to use the parts of speech notations to show how the phrase fits the pattern: preposition + noun/pronoun, no verb. Answer: *against … remedy* (*my* is a pronoun).

Style

Have your students choose the single best of the following dress-ups from this week's sentences. Discuss their answers. Best possibilities:

Strong verbs. *judged, indicated, pressed.*

Quality adjectives. *cunning, enlarged.*

-ly adverbs. *rightly, heavily.*

remedy: something that cures; a healing medicine

Check comprehension of **pressed**, meaning he urged her or pressured her for an answer.

STUDENT REWRITE

The soldier rightly judged, "I must frighten this cunning princess a little more if I'm to get what I want from her."

Thus, he left her with another large dose of the apple and indicated he would call on the morrow.

The next day the princess's enlarged nose was worse than before.

"My noble lady," pressed the doctor, "something works too heavily against my remedy.

Week 31

Review

LEARN IT

There are no new concepts for today. See if you can answer the questions below. If not, check your grammar cards for the answers.

- When do you use *its* and when do you use *it's*?
- Use each in a sentence.

Do you remember what these vocabulary words mean? If not, look them up in your vocabulary list in the back of your notebook.

- bizarre
- queried
- inspected
- assist
- chuckled

Be very careful with quotation marks! There can be several sentences within one set of quotation marks.

FIX IT

Read   Read the sentence.

Vocabulary   Look up the bolded word in a dictionary and decide which definition best fits the meaning of the word in this sentence. Add the definition to the list in the back of your notebook.

Day 1   Your teacher will help you mark and fix the first passage. Complete the rewrite after fixing.

Days 2–4   Use the abbreviations at the top of the next page and the grammar cards to help you remember how to mark the passage. Your teacher will help you with anything you miss. Remember, a mistake is an opportunity to learn. Continue to evaluate the dress-ups used this week. Out of all the choices, circle the single strongest verb, adjective, and -ly adverb.

Rewrite   Copy the corrected passage into a separate notebook.
- Be sure to double-space and indent where indicated.
- Do not copy the markings, just the story.
- Remember to use capital letters properly.
- Carefully copy the punctuation and use end marks.

Page 64, *Fix It! Grammar:* **The Nose Tree, Student Book 1**

DAY 1

pr	n	vb	pr		pr	vb	vb	adj	n	prep	pr

<u>my</u> **arts** inform me that you must have stolen property <u>about you</u>.

Fixes

Indent. Is this a new topic, speaker, place, or time? Answer: No. The soldier is still speaking to the princess.

Quotations. No quotation marks because the soldier is still speaking. Do not close quotations until the end of his speech (Day 2).

Capitalization. Capitalize the first word of a sentence.

End marks. Period at end of statement.

Grammar Notations

Pronouns. If your students do not label *my*, explain that it is another possessive pronoun. It is not in their list of pronouns to look for because it occurs infrequently in *Nose Tree*.

Verbs. *inform, must have.* Ask: Which of these are helping verbs? Answer: *must*, which helps out *have*. *Have* is an action verb here meaning possess, not a helping verb.

Adjectives. *stolen.* If this confuses students, point out that it describes the noun *property* so must be an adjective.

♡ **Grammar lovers.** Past participles like *stolen* often function as adjectives.

Prepositional phrases. *about you.* Ask students to use the parts of speech notations to show how the phrase fits the pattern: preposition + noun/pronoun, no verb.

arts: skill attained by study or observation. This lesser-known definition of *arts* may be hard to find in some dictionaries, so guide your students.

Check that students understand that **property** here does not mean land but something owned.

DAY 2

don't

cl	pr	vb		vb	ar	adj		n	pr	vb	vb		n	prep	pr

if you ~~do not~~ restore the **pilfered** goods, i̱ can do naught <u>for you</u>."

Fixes

Indent. Is this a new topic, speaker, place, or time? Answer: No. This continues and finishes the soldier's words to the princess.

Capitalization. Capitalize the first word of a sentence and the personal pronoun *I*.

Apostrophes. In their rewrite, have students form *do not* into its contraction *don't*. Remind them that contractions work well in stories, especially in dialogue, but usually not in formal papers.

End marks. Period at end of statement inside closing quotations. Check that students finished his speech with the closing quotations.

pilfered: stolen

Check that students understand the meaning of **goods**: with an *s*, it is a noun meaning *possessions*.

Naught means nothing.

Grammar Notations

Verbs. *do restore, can do.*

Ask: Which of these are helping verbs? Answer: *do*, which helps out *restore*, and *can*, which helps *do*. If students are confused by *do*, explain that it is a helping verb only when followed by an action verb. If it is the second of two verbs, it is the action verb itself.

♡ **Grammar lovers.** *not* is an adverb, not part of the verb.

Adjectives. *pilfered*. If students do not see this as an adjective, point out that it describes the noun *goods* and therefore must be an adjective.

♡ **Grammar lovers.** This is a verbal (the past participle of the verb *pilfer*) that functions as an adjective.

Prepositional phrases. *for you.* Ask students to use the parts of speech notations to show how the phrase fits the pattern: preposition + noun/pronoun, no verb.

Clause starters. *If.* From the parts of speech notations, show that there is a subject (noun or pronoun) and verb after this clause starter: *If you do not restore.*

DAY 3

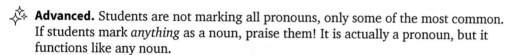

¶ the princess **stoutly** denied that she possessed anything of the kind.

Fixes

Indent. Is this a new topic, speaker, place, or time? Answer: Yes. Start a new paragraph because of a new topic, pulling out of speech and turning attention to the princess's response.

Capitalization. Capitalize the first word of a sentence.

End marks. Period at end of statement.

Grammar Notations

Articles and nouns. *The princess, the kind.*

Pronouns. *she.*

> ✦ **Advanced.** Students are not marking all pronouns, only some of the most common. If students mark *anything* as a noun, praise them! It is actually a pronoun, but it functions like any noun.

-ly adverbs. *stoutly.* Ask: What part of speech does this adverb describe? Answer: the verb *denied.*

Prepositional phrases. *of the kind.* Ask students to use the parts of speech notations to show how the phrase fits the pattern: preposition + noun/pronoun, no verb: *of ... kind.*

stoutly: stubbornly; forcefully

Note that *stoutly* can mean *boldly* or *bravely*, but since she is concealing something stolen, the context requires the more negative meaning.

DAY 4

pr vb pr   n   vb   ar   n   ly   pr   vb   vb   cl   pr

¶   "~~its~~/it's your choice," replied the doctor **casually**. "you may do as you

I'm

vb   cc   pr   vb   adj   pr   vb   adj

please, but ~~i am~~ sure i am unmistaken."

Fixes

Indent. Is this a new topic, speaker, place, or time? Answer: Yes. Start a new paragraph because of a new speaker.

Capitalization. Capitalize the first word of a sentence and the personal pronoun *I*.

Usage. Have students cross out the in correct *its/it's*, explain the meaning of the correct one, and check the spelling when copied. This should be *it's* for the contraction: *it is* your choice, or *it's* your choice.

Apostrophes. In their rewrite, have students form the first *I am* into its contraction *I'm*. Remind them that contractions work well in stories, especially in dialogue, but usually not in formal papers. Note: It is fine if they convert both to *I'm*, but it sounds a little smoother to keep the second as two words.

End marks. Period at end of statement inside closing quotations.

Grammar Notations

Pronouns. If your students do not label *your*, explain that it is another possessive pronoun. It is not in their list of pronouns to look for because it occurs only once in *Nose Tree*.

Verbs. *is* (in *It's*), *replied, may do, please, am, am*. If students do not recognize *am* as a verb, show them a list of *be* verbs (*am, is, are, was, were*) and ask them to find them. Ask: Which of these are helping verbs? Answer: *may*, which helps out *do*.

-ly adverbs. *casually*. Ask: What part of speech does this adverb describe? Answer: the verb *replied*. This is another situation where the adverb comes after the verb it describes.

Coordinating conjunctions. *but*.

> ✧ **Advanced.** Ask what words the cc *but* joins. Answer: two main clauses. Main clauses have a subject and verb and can stand alone as a sentence.

Clause starters. *as*. From the parts of speech notations, show that there is a subject (noun or pronoun) and verb after this clause starter: as *you please*.

Style

Have your students choose the single best of the following dress-ups from this week's sentences. Discuss their answers. Best possibilities:

Strong verbs. *restore, denied, possessed, replied*.

Quality adjectives. *stolen, pilfered, unmistaken*.

-ly adverbs. *stoutly, casually*.

casually: seeming to be unconcerned or indifferent about what is happening

Check that students understand that **unmistaken** means *correct; not in error*.

✏ **Teacher's note.** Students may mark *sure* or *unmistaken* as verbs, but these are adjectives called subject complements, which come after linking verbs (*am*) and describe the subject (*I*). See Grammar Glossary: Parts of Speech: Verbs: Linking Verbs: page G-8, and Parts of Speech: Adjectives, page G-10.

STUDENT REWRITE

Since this passage continues without another indentation, be sure students continue writing where last week's passage left off.

My arts inform me that you must have stolen property about you. If you don't restore the pilfered goods, I can do naught for you."

The princess stoutly denied that she possessed anything of the kind.

"It's your choice," replied the doctor casually. "You may do as you please, but I'm sure I am unmistaken."

Week 32

Discuss the Learn It part with your students.

Adjust the lessons as needed.

This week is a review week.

Review

LEARN IT

There are no new concepts for today. See if you can answer the questions below. If not, check your grammar cards for the answers.

- When do you use *your* and when do you use *you're*?
- Use each in a sentence.

Do you remember what these vocabulary words mean? If not, look them up in your vocabulary list in the back of your notebook.

- flourished
- genial
- obtain
- heartily
- exquisite

FIX IT

Read	Read the sentence.
Vocabulary	Look up the bolded word in a dictionary and decide which definition best fits the meaning of the word in this sentence. Add the definition to the list in the back of your notebook.
Day 1	Your teacher will help you mark and fix the first passage. Complete the rewrite after fixing.
Days 2–4	Use the abbreviations at the top of the next page and the grammar cards to help you remember how to mark the passage. Your teacher will help you with anything you miss. Remember, a mistake is an opportunity to learn. Continue to evaluate the dress-ups used this week. Out of all the choices, circle the single strongest verb, adjective, and -ly adverb.
Rewrite	Copy the corrected passage into a separate notebook.

- Be sure to double-space and indent where indicated.
- Do not copy the markings, just the story.
- Remember to use capital letters properly.
- Carefully copy the punctuation and use end marks.

Page 66, *Fix It! Grammar:* The Nose Tree, Student Book 1

DAY 1

>   *ar*   *n*   *vb* *prep ar*   *n*   *cc*   *ly*   *vb*   *prep pr*   *ar*
> ¶ the soldier hurried <u>to the king</u> and plainly **published** <u>to him</u> how the
>
>   *n*   *vb*
> matter stood.

Fixes

published: made publicly known

Indent. Is this a new topic, speaker, place, or time? Answer: Yes. Start a new paragraph because of a new topic, pulling out of speech and turning to the soldier's actions.

Capitalization. Capitalize the first word of a sentence.

End marks. Period at end of statement.

Grammar Notations

-ly adverbs. *plainly*. Ask: What part of speech does this adverb describe? Answer: the verb *published*.

Prepositional phrases. *to the king, to him*. Ask students to use the parts of speech notations to show how each phrase fits the pattern: preposition + noun/pronoun, no verb: *to … king, to him*.

Coordinating conjunctions. *and*.

> ✧ **Advanced.** Ask what words the cc *and* joins. Answer: two verbs, *hurried* and *published*.

DAY 2

¶   *n*   *vb*   *ar*   *n*   *vb*   *prep*   *pr*

¶   "<u>d</u>aughter," commanded the king, "return to ~~there~~/their/~~they're~~

adj   *n*   *ar*   *n*   *ar*   *n*   *cc*   *ar*   *n*

legitimate <u>owners</u> the cloak, the purse, and the horn, ~~to/two/~~too."

Fixes

legitimate: lawful; rightful

Indent. Is this a new topic, speaker, place, or time? Answer: Yes. Start a new paragraph because of a new speaker.

Capitalization. Capitalize the first word of a sentence.

Homophones and usage. Have students cross out the incorrect *there/their/they're* and *to/two/too* and check the spelling when copied.

> Ask: Which words does *their* refer to? Answer: *cloak, purse, horn.*

> Ask: What does *too* mean in this sentence? Answer: also.

Quotation. Check that students copy the quotation marks correctly. Remind them that when narrative (*commanded the king*) interrupts speech, the narrative is set off with commas. Also, point out that *return* is lowercase because it is a continuation of his sentence.

End marks. Period at end of statement.

Grammar Notations

Prepositional phrases. *to their legitimate owners.* Ask students to use the parts of speech notations to show how the phrase fits the pattern: preposition + noun/ pronoun, no verb: *to ... owners.*

Coordinating conjunctions. *and.*

> Ask: What words does this cc join? Answer: This time it is three nouns, not two: *cloak, purse,* and *horn.*

> Also, show that commas are needed when there are three or more items in a series.

DAY 3

adj	ar	n	vb	pr	n	adj	w-w	pr

¶ defeated, the princess ordered her maid to **fetch** all three, which she

vb	vb	prep	pr	adj	n	cl	vb

had hidden in her private chamber where no one ever looked.

Fixes

fetch: go and return with

Indent. Is this a new topic, speaker, place, or time? Answer: Yes. Start a new paragraph because of a new topic, pulling out of speech and turning to the princess's response.

Capitalization. Capitalize the first word of a sentence.

End marks. Period at end of statement.

Grammar Notations

Articles and nouns. *the princess, maid, chamber.*

> ✦ **Advanced.** Students do not need to catch the noun *three* or pronoun *no one*. *Three* is usually an adjective but must then have a noun after it that it describes; here, it is a noun. *No one* means *no person* and is a pronoun.

Verbs. *ordered, had hidden, looked.* Ask: Which of these are helping verbs? Answer: *had,* which helps out *hidden.*

> ✦ **Advanced.** Accept it if students mark the infinitive *to fetch* as a verb since it expresses an action even though technically it is not a verb.

Adjectives. *Defeated, all, private.*

> ♡ **Grammar lovers.** If students mark *defeated* as a verb instead of as an adjective, let it go. *Defeated* is a verbal, the past participle of the verb *to defeat.* Since it is not used with a helping verb ("she was defeated," for example), it is not functioning as a verb but as an adjective modifying *princess.*

> ✦ **Advanced.** Students may not catch that *all* functions as an adjective in this sentence describing the noun *three.* It is not critical that they recognize this now.

Prepositional phrases. *in her private chamber.* Ask students to use the parts of speech notations to show how the phrase fits the pattern: preposition + noun/ pronoun, no verb: *in … chamber.*

***Who-which* clauses.** Read the entire clause aloud: *which she had hidden in her private chamber.* Ask: What noun immediately before it does this *which* clause describe? Answer: *three* (all three items). Ask students to show you where the commas are placed (none at end).

Clause starters. *where.* From the parts of speech notations, show that there is a subject (noun or pronoun) and verb after this clause starter: where *no one* ever *looked.*

✎ **Teacher's note.** You do not need to discuss everything on this page with your student. Limit these lessons to fifteen minutes per day. The goal is repetition, but every detail does not need to be repeated every day.

DAY 4

pr	ly	vb	pr	prep	ar	n	cc	vb	pr		pr	prep	ar

<u>s</u>he **crossly** handed them <u>to the doctor</u> and urged him to return them <u>to the</u>

adj	n

<u>rightful owners</u>.

Fixes

Indent. Is this a new topic, speaker, place, or time? Answer: No, because it continues to tell about the princess's defeat.

Capitalization. Capitalize the first word of a sentence.

End marks. Period at end of statement.

crossly: in an ill-humored or irritable manner

Check that your students understand the meaning of **urged**: to try to persuade; to beg.

Grammar Notations

Verbs. *handed, urged*. If students mark the infinitive *to return* as a verb, accept it.

-ly adverbs. *crossly*. Ask: What part of speech does this adverb describe? Answer: the verb *handed*.

Prepositional phrases. *to the doctor, to the rightful owners*. Ask students to use the parts of speech notations to show how each phrase fits the pattern: preposition + noun/pronoun, no verb: *to … doctor; to … owners*.

Coordinating conjunctions. *and*. Ask: What words does this cc join? Answer: two verbs, *handed* and *urged*.

Style

Have your students choose the single best of the following dress-ups from this week's sentences. Discuss their answers. Best possibilities:

Strong verbs. *hurried, published, commanded, ordered, urged.*

Quality adjectives. *legitimate, rightful.*

-ly adverbs. *plainly, crossly.*

STUDENT REWRITE

The soldier hurried to the king and plainly published to him how the matter stood.

"Daughter," commanded the king, "return to their legitimate owners the cloak, the purse, and the horn, too."

Defeated, the princess ordered her maid to fetch all three, which she had hidden in her private chamber where no one ever looked. She crossly handed them to the doctor and urged him to return them to the rightful owners.

Week 33

Review

LEARN IT

There are no new concepts for today. See if you can answer the questions below. If not, check your grammar cards for the answers.

- Name the two reasons that a word should start with a capital letter.
- Can you remember what words are coordinating conjunctions? (Hint: FANBOYS)

Do you remember what these vocabulary words mean? If not, look them up in your vocabulary list in the back of your notebook.

- gobbled
- spacious
- modest
- judged
- pilfered

FIX IT

Read	Read the sentence.
Vocabulary	Look up the bolded word in a dictionary and decide which definition best fits the meaning of the word in this sentence. Add the definition to the list in the back of your notebook.
Day 1	Your teacher will help you mark and fix the first passage. Complete the rewrite after fixing.
Days 2–4	Use the abbreviations at the top of the next page and the grammar cards to help you remember how to mark the passage. Your teacher will help you with anything you miss. Remember, a mistake is an opportunity to learn. Continue to evaluate the dress-ups used this week. Out of all the choices, circle the single strongest verb, adjective, and -ly adverb.
Rewrite	Copy the corrected passage into a separate notebook.

- Be sure to double-space and indent where indicated.
- Do not copy the markings, just the story.
- Remember to use capital letters properly.
- Carefully copy the punctuation and use end marks.

Page 68, *Fix It! Grammar:* The Nose Tree, Student Book 1

DAY 1

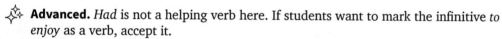

      cl   *ar*   *n*   *vb*   *pr*   *adj*   *prep* *pr*   *n*   *pr*   *vb*   *pr* *ar*

¶ when the soldier had them **secure** in his possession, he presented her a

   adj   *n*

whole pear to enjoy.

Fixes

secure: safe; in safe keeping

Indent. Is this a new topic, speaker, place, or time? Answer: Yes. Start a new paragraph because of a new topic, the soldier's true cure.

Capitalization. Capitalize the first word of a sentence.

End marks. Period at end of statement.

Grammar Notations

Verbs. *had, presented.*

   ⁂ **Advanced.** *Had* is not a helping verb here. If students want to mark the infinitive *to enjoy* as a verb, accept it.

Prepositional phrases. *in his possession.* Ask students to use the parts of speech notations to show how the phrase fits the pattern: preposition + noun/pronoun, no verb: *in … possession.*

Clause starters. *When.* From the parts of speech notations, show that there is a subject (noun or pronoun) and verb after this clause starter (subordinating conjunction): When the *soldier had.*

DAY 2

ly   pr   n   w-w prep   n   vb   ly   vb   prep pr   adj

<u>fi</u>nally, her nose, which <u>**by now**</u> ached miserably, returned <u>to its ~~it's~~ **natural**</u>

n

<u>size</u>.

Fixes

natural: as it was
formed by nature

Indent. Is this a new topic, speaker, place, or time? Answer: No, because the sentence is still about her cure.

Capitalization. Capitalize the first word of a sentence.

Usage. Have students cross out the incorrect *its/it's*, explain the meaning of the correct word, and check the spelling when copied. This should be *its* expressing possession: the size of the nose, or its size.

End marks. Period at end of statement.

Grammar Notations

Articles and nouns. *nose, now, size.* If your students do not catch *now*, let it go. It is usually an adverb but sometimes a noun. You could point out that it means "this moment," which is more obviously a noun. It also comes after a preposition, which must have a noun at the end of its phrase.

Verbs. *ached, returned.*

  ✧ **Advanced.** Ask, What word in the sentence is the subject of *returned*?
     Answer: *nose.*

  ♡ **Grammar lovers.** The *which* clause comes between the first subject and its verb (*nose returned*). The subject of *ached* is *which.*

-ly adverbs. *Finally, miserably.* Ask: What part of speech does the adverb *miserably* describe? Answer: *miserably* modifies *ached.*

  ✧ **Advanced.** What part of speech does the adverb *finally* describe? *Finally* modifies *returned* (*finally returned*).

Prepositional phrases. *by now, to its natural size.* Ask students to use the parts of speech notations to show how each phrase fits the pattern: preposition + noun/ pronoun, no verb: *by now; to … size.*

***Who-which* clauses.** Read the entire clause aloud: *which by now ached miserably.* Ask: What noun immediately before it does this *which* clause describe? Answer: *nose.* Ask students to show you where the commas are placed.

DAY 3

	ar	n	vb	ar	n	vb	ar	n	cc	pr	n		n		cc

¶ the doctor put on the cloak, wished the king and his court farewell, and

vb	prep	pr	adj		n		ly

was with his ~~to~~ two ~~too~~ companions **directly**.

Fixes

directly: shortly;
without delay

Indent. Is this a new topic, speaker, place, or time? Answer: Yes. Start a new paragraph because of a new topic, the soldier's return to his companions.

Capitalization. Capitalize the first word of a sentence.

Homophones. Have students cross out the incorrect *to/two/too* and check the spelling when copied.

End marks. Period at end of statement.

Grammar Notations

Articles and nouns. *The doctor, the cloak, the king, court, farewell, companions.*

> ✧ **Advanced.** Students may not catch *farewell*, which is fine. It is a noun here meaning good wishes expressed at parting.

Verbs. *put* (*put on* means to be clothed), *wished, was.* If students miss *was*, show them a list of *be* verbs (*am, is, are, was, were*) and ask them to find one.

> ✧ **Advanced.** If students ask, point out that *was* is not a helping verb here because there is no verb right after it.

-ly adverbs. *directly.* Ask: What part of speech does this adverb describe? Answer: the verb *was.*

Prepositional phrases. *with his two companions.* Ask students to use the parts of speech notations to show how the phrase fits the pattern: preposition + noun/pronoun, no verb: *with ... companions.*

> ✧ **Advanced.** If students mark *on the cloak* as a prepositional phrase, it is fine. You could explain that as a prepositional phrase, *on the cloak* indicates that something is on the cloak, as in "he put a pin on the cloak." In the Day 3 sentence, *put on* makes sense and *on the cloak* does not.

Coordinating conjunctions. *and, and.*

Ask: What words do these cc's join? Answer: The first joins two nouns, *king* and *court.*

The second joins three verbs, *put on, wished,* and *was.* Show that all three verbs use the same subject (*doctor*) and that these items in a series are separated by commas because there are three or more of them.

DAY 4

prep *adj* *n* *ar* *n* *vb* *ly* *prep* *n* *prep* *pr*
from that time the soldiers lived cheerfully at home in ~~there~~/their ~~/they're~~

n *cc* *ly* *vb* *ar* *n* *ar* *n* *prep*
palace and occasionally took an **airing** to discover the world in

pr *n* *prep* *ar* *adj* *adj* *n*
~~there~~/their ~~/they're~~ coach with the three dapple-gray horses.

Fixes

airing: a drive out in the open air

Indent. Is this a new topic, speaker, place, or time? Answer: No, because it continues to talk about what happened afterward.

Capitalization. Capitalize the first word of a sentence.

Homophones. Have students cross out the incorrect *there/their/they're* (two places) and check the spelling when copied.

End marks. Period at end of statement.

Grammar Notations

Verbs. *lived, took.* If students mark the infinitive *to discover* as a verb, accept it.

-ly adverbs. *cheerfully, occasionally.* Ask: What part of speech do these adverbs describe? Answer: the verbs *lived* and *took*.

Prepositional phrases. *From that time, at home, in their palace, in their coach, with the three dapple-gray horses.* Ask students to use the parts of speech notations to show how each phrase fits the pattern: preposition + noun/pronoun, no verb: *from … time; at home; in … palace; in … coach; with … horses.*

Coordinating conjunction. *and.* Ask: What words does this cc join? Answer: the verbs *lived* and *took.* The same noun (*soldiers*) has two verbs.

Style

Have your students choose the single best of the following dress-ups from this week's sentences. Discuss their answers. Best possibilities:

Strong verbs. *presented, ached.*

Quality adjectives. *secure, natural, dapple-gray.*

-ly adverbs. *miserably, directly, cheerfully.*

STUDENT REWRITE

When the soldier had them secure in his possession, he presented her a whole pear to enjoy. Finally, her nose, which by now ached miserably, returned to its natural size.

The doctor put on the cloak, wished the king and his court farewell, and was with his two companions directly. From that time the soldiers lived cheerfully at home in their palace and occasionally took an airing to discover the world in their coach with the three dapple-gray horses.

Scope and Sequence

Week	Parts of Speech	Punctuation	Dress-Ups	Homophones and Usage	Other Concepts	Vocabulary
1	Nouns (n)	End marks		There, their, they're	Indent (¶)	poor destitute wretched gloomy
2	Articles (ar)					keeping watch alert dwarf rebuffing
3		Quotations				plight worthy comrades don
4	Pronouns (pr)					elfin in due time likewise sociable
5	*Which* clauses (w-w)					purse awarding graciously curious
6	*Who* clauses (w-w)					dumbfounded survey settle down wondrous
7	Action verbs (vb)					trice encircled abundant dapple-gray
8			Identify possible strong verbs			splendid dwell neighboring elegant
9		Apostrophes to show ownership (possessives)				crafty observant luxuriant roamed
10	Helping verbs (vb)					rashly confided cunning indistinguishable
11		Apostrophes with contractions				banquet substituted bade farewell enclosed

Institute for Excellence in Writing

Week	Parts of Speech	Punctuation	Dress-Ups	Homophones and Usage	Other Concepts	Vocabulary
12					Indentation rules	divulged suspected chamber tallying
13		Exclamation points		To, two, too		lingered pivoted rattled ordinarily
14	Adjectives (adj)					vacate vaulted haste covetous
15			Identify possible quality adjectives			despair vibrated immense besieged
16					Capitals	demolished challenged countered ploy
17	-ly Adverbs (ly)		Identify strongest -ly adverb			masqueraded crept ballads preoccupied
18				Its versus It's		disbanded invaluable forlorn mournfully
19	Prepositions (prep)					determined drifted fortune bone-weary
20					Review questions: articles and nouns	laden plucked peculiar detected
21	Coordinating conjunctions (cc)					cease arched inch on dale
22					Review questions: verbs and coordinating conjunctions	meantime bizarre queried inspected

Scope and Sequence

Week	Parts of Speech	Punctuation	Dress-Ups	Homophones and Usage	Other Concepts	Vocabulary
23	Clause starters (cl) www.asia.b					elongated pitiable assist in vain
24					Review questions: adjectives and clause starters	benefactor chuckled antidote flourished
25				Your/You're		rightful genial feast obtain
26					Review questions: pronouns	heartily undertake costumed exquisite
27					Review questions: helping verbs	appointed gobbled spacious appalling
28					Review questions: apostrophes	alleviate sprucely restore humbled
29					Comparative adjectives	dose anticipated modest meddle
30					Review questions: prepositions	judged morrow enlarged remedy
31					Review questions: *its* and *it's*	arts pilfered stoutly casually
32					Review questions: *your* and *you're*	published legitimate fetch crossly
33					Review questions: capital letters and cc's	secure natural directly airing

Institute for Excellence in Writing

Fix It!
Grammar

Glossary

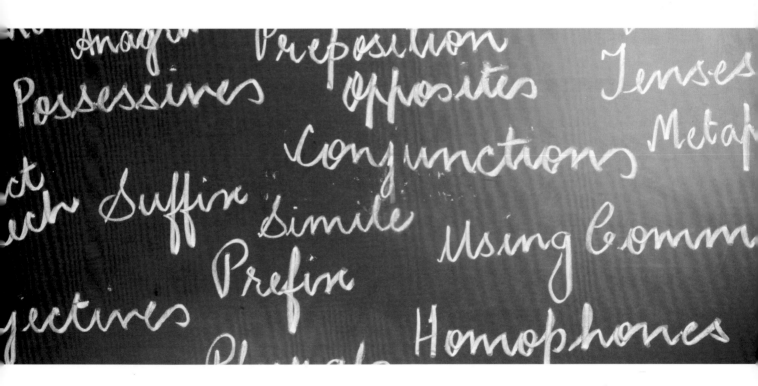

Pamela White

Institute for
Excellence in
Writing

Listen. Speak. Read. Write. Think!

Fix It!
Grammar

Glossary

Pamela White

THIRD EDITION

Contents

Making grammar friendly

This glossary is available for reference if you wish to refresh your memory or would like more information about a specific rule.

One goal of the Institute for Excellence in Writing is to make grammar friendly for younger students and beginning writers. Thus, the terms used in the early *Fix It! Grammar* books are layman's terms, such as *-ing opener* instead of participle and *who-which* instead of adjective clause.

However, grammar terms are useful to the teacher and the student over time, so they are gradually incorporated into the books as well as defined in the glossary.

With the repetition provided in the Fix Its, your students will learn the elements and rules of grammar in manageable increments.

Editing Marks

indent	¶
capitalize	≡
lowercase	/
delete	ℓ
insert	∨
space	#
close up	‿

Parts of Speech

Many words can be used as different parts of speech. You have to look at how they are used in the sentence to determine their parts of speech. To see how these parts of speech are used as IEW dress-ups and sentence openers, see the Stylistic Techniques section beginning on page G-35.

Articles (ar)

Articles are the words *a, an, the.*

Articles always set up a noun, so when students see an article, they should know that a noun will follow soon after. Sometimes adjectives come between the article and its noun: *a tall stranger; the reluctant, timid soldier.*

Nouns (n)

Nouns are objects (things), people, animals, places, and ideas.

To determine if a word is a noun, apply these two tests, which work best for objects and animals:

    1. Is it countable? *two* _____

    2. Can an article come in front of it? *the* _____; *a/an* _____.

Common and Proper Nouns

Common nouns name general things and are not capitalized.

Proper nouns are capitalized and name specific people, places, animals, and sometimes objects with a name unique to that specific person, place, or animal. *The king* is a common noun, but *King James* is proper. A *beagle* is a common noun, but the name of my pet beagle *Benji* is proper.

Compound Nouns

These are two or more words combined to form a single noun. They can be written as separate words (*apple tree; shooting match*), as hyphenated words (*lady-in-waiting*), or as one word (*marksman; wintertime*). To spell compound words correctly, consult a dictionary.

Students may be confused how to use something like *apple tree* in key word outlines or in marking nouns. A compound noun is not an adjective + noun or two nouns but just a single noun. These are nouns that could have been written as a single word because they express a single thing.

Noun Functions

The two functions of nouns and pronouns that are most useful to understand are the subject and the object of a preposition.

Subjects are nouns or pronouns that perform a verb action. Identify subjects by finding the verb first and then asking, "Who or what is doing this action?" That is the subject.

Saying that a noun is a subject identifies how it functions or behaves in that sentence; it is different from the part of speech (noun or pronoun).

Subject-verb agreement means that the subject and its verb should agree in number. If the subject is singular, the verb should be singular; if the subject is plural, the verb should be plural. Students occasionally find it confusing that a singular verb often ends in *s* and a plural verb does not: *she walks* but *they walk*.

The **object of a preposition** is the noun or pronoun that is the last word in a prepositional phrase. See under Parts of Speech: Prepositions, page G-11; and Stylistic Techniques: Sentence Openers: #2 Prepositional Opener, page G-39.

Other Noun Functions (Advanced)

Direct and **indirect objects** are important mainly as they relate to pronoun usage (*The soldier treated him graciously*, not *The soldier treated he graciously*). Since these are objects, they must use objective pronouns (see under Pronouns on the next page).

Direct objects follow a verb and answer the question *what* or *who*. Example: *The third soldier built a fire.* Built what? *a fire* (direct object).

Indirect objects are rarer and appear only when there is a direct object. They usually come between the verb and direct object and tell who or what received the direct object. Example: *The little man gave the second soldier a purse.* Gave what? *the purse* (direct object). Who received it? *the soldier* (indirect object).

The difficulty is that indirect objects also seem to answer the question *who* or *what* (gave who? *the soldier*). Tip: To tell the difference, you should be able to insert *to* in front of the indirect object: *gave a purse to the second soldier*. He is not giving the soldier to someone else.

Subject complements, a.k.a. predicate nouns, are important for the same pronoun usage problem (*It was she*, not *It was her*). These are nouns that follow a linking verb and point back to the subject, so they *complement* the subject.

Subject complements use subjective, not objective, pronouns (see under Pronouns on the next page), which is the only reason to teach these to older students. Note: Adjectives can also be subject complements.

Appositives are nouns that rename the noun that comes before them. They are important because they are punctuated with commas if nonessential (*Robin Hood, the archer*) and without commas if essential (*the archer Robin Hood*).

> **Imperative mood** is used to issue commands. The subject, *you*, is implied.
>
> Example: *Tarry for me here.* Robin Hood is addressing his men, asking them to wait for him. *You* is the implied subject.

Pronouns (pr)

Personal pronouns refer back to a person or thing recently mentioned and substitute for that person or thing. They should agree in case, person, and number with the noun they refer to. Begin with having students identify basic pronouns and later work on pronoun agreement.

There are three cases:

Subjective case pronouns are used as the subject (or, infrequently, subject complements).

Objective case pronouns are used as objects of verbs or prepositions.

Possessive case pronouns show ownership. These do not have an apostrophe.

	Subjective pronouns	Objective pronouns	Possessive pronouns
1st person singular	I	me	my/mine
2nd person singular	you	you	your/yours
3rd person singular	he, she, it	him, her, it	his, her/hers, its
1st person plural	we	us	our/ours
2nd person plural	you	you	your/yours
3rd person plural	they	them	their/theirs
	who	whom	whose

Pronoun agreement: To agree in person means that first person pronouns should not shift suddenly to second or third. To agree in number means that a singular pronoun should refer back to a singular noun and a plural pronoun should refer to a plural noun.

There are several different categories of pronouns in addition to personal pronouns (relative, demonstrative, interrogative, indefinite, reflexive), but in practice, teach them only as they become relevant in writing.

Reflexive pronouns end in *self* or *selves* and refer back to a noun or pronoun in the same sentence.

Examples:

Princess Dorinda fancied *herself* quite chic.

The fish allowed *themselves* to be stroked.

Verbs (vb)

Verbs are words that express either action or a state of being. There are three types: action, linking, and helping verbs.

Action Verbs

Action verbs express action (as in *chop, budge, confide*) or ownership (as in *have, possess, own*).

Verb + Adverb (Advanced)

In identifying parts of speech, some students are confused by what look like prepositions after a verb but without the usual noun afterward. In this case, these words do not function as prepositions but as adverbs that must be coupled with that verb.

Examples: *Robin Hood set off; the Merry Men rose up; they cavorted about; stand back.*

Helping Verbs

Helping verbs appear with action verbs to help them along. Picture the helping verb as a Boy Scout who helps an elderly lady cross the street. One helps the other along!

Examples: *The magical purse would always refill with gold. Would* helps *refill. She had played him a trick. Had* helps out *played.*

Tip: Helping verbs communicate possibility (*can, could, might*, etc.) or time (*was, did, has*, etc.).

Helping verbs:

> *am, is, are, was, were, be, being, been* (*be* verbs, which can also be linking verbs)
>
> *have, has, had*
>
> *do, does, did*
>
> *may, might, must, ought to*
>
> *would, will, could, can, should, shall*

Linking Verbs

Linking verbs connect the subject to a noun or adjective that renames or describes it and is called the **subject complement** (a.k.a. predicate noun and predicate adjective).

Examples: *Robin Hood was* (linking verb) *an outlaw* (subject complement). *The combatants seemed* (linking verb) *weary* (subject complement). *The princess was* (linking verb) *artful and cunning* (subject complements).

Common linking verbs:

> *am, is, are, was, were, be, being, been* (*be* verbs, which can also be helping verbs)
>
> *seem, become* (always linking verbs)
>
> *appear, grow, remain, continue*
>
> *taste, sound, smell, feel, look* (verbs dealing with the senses)

Some of these verbs can also be action verbs. Tip: If you can substitute *seem* for the verb, it is probably a linking verb.

Be Verbs

Be verbs often stump students when identifying parts of speech because they do not show action. Since they dominate our language and perform important functions as helping and linking verbs, it is important students can recognize that they are verbs.

Ask students to memorize the *be* verbs: *am, is, are, was, were, be, being, been.*

Verbals: Infinitives, Participles, Gerunds (Advanced)

Verbals are words formed from a verb, but they usually do not function as a verb.

You do not have to teach students to identify whether a particular verbal is functioning as a noun or adjective or adverb. There is little point to drilling this harder concept except to mention that verbals are not verbs. Learning what function they take will not affect punctuation or help most students understand grammar, nor will it show up on the SAT or ACT.

As a strong verb dress-up? If students want to label a verbal as a strong verb, decide whether it is too advanced to direct them toward basic action verbs instead.

It helps older students to have a basic understanding of these verbals:

1. Infinitives are verbals formed by placing *to* in front of the simple present form of a verb (like *to sneeze*). Infinitives function as adjectives, adverbs, and nouns but never as verbs.

2. Participles often function as adjectives and come in two forms: present (-ing words) and past participles (-ed words). However, when participles are coupled with a subject and a helping verb, they function as verbs, as in *He **was splashing**, which frightened the fish. For years, she **had longed** to visit the world above the sea.*

> **a.** Sometimes these participle-adjectives appear directly before the noun: *hunting skills; a botched case.*

> **b.** Sometimes they are an -ing or -ed phrase coming before or after a main clause and modifying the subject of the main clause: *Springing to his feet, Robin Hood confronted the challenger.* (*Springing* describes *Robin Hood*, the subject after the comma.) See under Stylistic Techniques: Sentence Openers: #4 -ing Participial Phrase Opener, page G-41.

3. Gerunds are -ing words that function as nouns. Examples: *His splashing frightened the fish.* (*Splashing* is the subject of the sentence and therefore a noun.) *The fish were frightened by his splashing.* (*Splashing* is the object of the preposition *by* and therefore a noun.)

Split infinitives

A concern more of the past than the present, *split infinitives* are worth teaching advanced writers. To split one's infinitive is to insert one or more adverbs between "to" and the verb, as in "to foolishly insert."

Generally, split infinitives are acceptable but formerly frowned on, so avoid them when it is just as smooth to place the intervening adverb somewhere else.

Adjectives (adj)

Adjectives are words that describe or modify nouns and pronouns. Usually they come before the noun they modify, as in *the crowded room* or *covetous princess*.

Sometimes adjectives come after a linking verb, as in *the princess was **thrilled**; the soldiers were **penniless** and **forlorn***.

Tip: When adjectives come after a linking verb, they are known as **subject complements** or **predicate adjectives**. See Parts of Speech: Verbs: Linking Verbs, page G-8.

Comparative and Superlative Adjectives

Comparative adjectives (ending in *-er*) and superlative adjectives (ending in *-est*) are forms of adjectives comparing two or more nouns. Students sometimes have trouble recognizing that words ending in *-er* or *-est* can be adjectives. Have them drop the ending and ask if the word remaining is an adjective.

Example: *The noblest buck is the most noble buck.* Drop the ending and ask if *noble* can describe a noun. It can, so *noble* and *noblest* are both adjectives.

Some words form irregular comparatives and superlatives. The most common of these are *good* and *bad*:

good, better, best

bad, worse, worst

Caution students against using *more* or *most* with a comparative or superlative adjective. Not *more prouder* but *prouder*. Most one-syllable adjectives form the comparative and superlative by adding the suffix. Adjectives of three or more syllables form the comparative with *more* and the superlative with *most* in front of the regular adjective. Two-syllable adjectives have more complex rules, but usually whichever sounds better is correct.

Adverbs (adv)

Adverbs usually modify verbs or adjectives and answer the questions *how, when,* or *where.* Encourage students to identify what part of speech the adverbs modify.

Example: *The princess stoutly denied that she possessed stolen goods. Stoutly* tells us how she denied, so it is the adverb, and it comes right before the verb it describes.

Many adverbs end in *-ly*. See Stylistic Techniques: Dress-Ups: -ly Adverb, page G-35; and Sentence Openers: #3 -ly Adverb Opener, page G-40.

Imposter -ly's: Some -ly words are adjectives like *chilly, ghastly, ugly,* and *friendly*. If the word describes an object or person (*the ugly duckling*), it is an adjective and not an adverb.

Advanced: Adverbs can also modify other adverbs, but this is rare and usually awkward in the hands of young writers, giving such unhelpful constructions as *she spoke extremely quickly.*

Advanced: Comparative adverbs are usually formed by adding *more* or *most* in front of the adverb. If the adverb is short, sometimes the suffix is used, as in *deadliest*. If in doubt, students should check a dictionary.

Prepositions (prep)

Prepositions start phrases that usually show some relationship dealing with space (*on the branch*) or time (*in the morning*). If it is something a frog can do with a log or a squirrel with a tree, it is probably a prepositional phrase: *climbs on the log, sits in the branches, runs around the tree.*

A prepositional phrase always follows this pattern:

preposition + noun (no verb)

It begins with a preposition, ends with a noun, and does not have a verb in it. Since there is not a subject + verb, it is a phrase, not a clause. There may be other words in between the preposition and noun, but there will never be a verb: *in the act; by a great baron; of strong and goodhearted yeomen.*

First learning parts of speech helps students accurately identify prepositional phrases. Until the concept is mastered, guide them to see that the phrase begins with a preposition, ends with a noun, and has no verb in it.

The most common prepositions:

aboard	at	despite	near	throughout
about	because of	down	of	to
above	before	during	off	toward
according to	behind	except	on, onto	under
across	below	for	opposite	underneath
after	beneath	from	out	unlike
against	beside	in	outside	until
along	besides	inside	over	unto
amid	between	instead of	past	up, upon
among	beyond	into	regarding	with
around	by	like	since	within
as	concerning	minus	through	without

In the first stories of *Fix It!* students are asked to identify prepositional phrases. Removing prepositional phrases helps students see the underlying structure of their sentences better, which is the basis for being able to punctuate correctly.

Doubling as other parts of speech: A few words in the preposition list are sometimes another part of speech, so guide students to determine this based on the pattern. The two most important examples:

1. Adverbs that follow a verb but do not start a prepositional phrase (*warded **off**; cried **out***).

2. Subordinating conjunctions that start dependent clauses: *since, as, until, after, before.* See under Stylistic Techniques: Sentence Openers: #5 Clausal Opener, page G-42.

Younger students do not need to count the preposition *to* in an infinitive, as in *to float*, since infinitives work a little differently from prepositional phrases.

On not ending sentences with prepositions: This is a carryover from Latin and not a true rule in English. Andrew Pudewa quips that Winston Churchill gave the definitive answer to this problem when he remarked, "That is a rule up with which I will not put!"

If the sentence is more awkward to revise with the preposition placed earlier, it is better to have it at the end. Example: *I have only a plain blackthorn staff to meet you with.* The alternative is this stilted construction: *I have only a plain blackthorn staff with which to meet you.*

Misplaced prepositional phrases: The later stories deal with the problem of dangling prepositional phrases where misplaced prepositional phrases distort the meaning, often humorously.

Example: ***King Arthur declared on special days*** *he would not feast until someone narrated a bizarre tale that he could trust.* The king did not make this declaration on special days; instead, he declared he would not feast on them.

Revise by moving the prepositional phrase: *King Arthur declared **he would not feast on special days** until someone narrated a bizarre tale that he could trust.*

Coordinating Conjunctions (cc)

Coordinating conjunctions connect parts of speech, phrases, and clauses. Whatever they connect needs to be the same thing grammatically: two or more nouns, two or more present participles, two or more dependent clauses, two or more main clauses, and so forth.

Have students memorize the seven basic coordinating conjunctions using the mnemonic device FANBOYS, an acronym for the cc's: *for, and, nor, but, or, yet, so.*

Punctuation: The main problem with cc's is that sometimes they have a comma in front of them and sometimes they do not. See Punctuation: Commas, page G-21.

The principles to keep in mind:

> **1.** Use commas before cc's when they join
>
> > **a.** two main clauses. Pattern: **MC, cc MC**. Example: *Usually Robin towered over others,* ***but*** *the stranger was taller by a head and a neck.*
> >
> > **b.** three or more items in a series. Pattern: **a, b, and c**. Example: *He ran to the window, opened it,* ***and*** *vaulted out.*
>
> **2.** Do not use commas before cc's when they join two items in a series unless those are MCs. Example: *fine gardens* ***and*** *wide lawns.*
>
> This applies to two verbs (a compound verb) with one subject. Pattern: **MC cc 2nd verb** (notice there is no comma). Example: *He bowed* ***and*** *walked away.*

Train students to locate cc's and then determine what same parts of speech or constructions they are joining. This matters because it shows whether or not the commas will be necessary: comma if three or more; no comma if only two unless MCs. It also matters because it helps students identify faulty parallelism. See sidebar.

Starting sentences with cc's: Strict grammarians forbid this on the basis that the job of cc's is to connect things of equal grammatical rank. Generally, encourage this avoidance, especially in academic papers, but it is not a hard and fast rule.

One clear exception is in dialogue, which can mimic real speech patterns. We often start our thoughts with *and* or *but.*

Faulty parallelism

Coordinating conjunctions should join parts of speech, phrases, or clauses of equal grammatical rank. When they do not, it is known as faulty parallelism, a concept middle and high school students should learn. It means that the items in a series are not parallel, that is, not the same part of speech, type of phrase, or type of clause.

Example: Once she **stole** into the throne room, **swinging** on the chandeliers, and **landed** at the feet of the scandalized courtiers.

Problem: The sentence sets up a parallel construction but is not consistent with its items in a series (bolded).

Corrected: Once she **stole** into the throne room, **swung** on the chandeliers, and **landed** at the feet of the scandalized courtiers.

Subordinating Conjunctions

In IEW's stylistic techniques, we begin by teaching students the because clause, then seven more common clause starters using the acronym **www.asia.b** for the words that can start dependent clauses:

when, while, where, as, since, if, although, because

Later we add three more:

until, whereas, unless

These are all subordinating conjunctions, so named because they start subordinate clauses, an older term for dependent clauses. There is no special need to teach the terminology (subordinating conjunction) except that it is important to distinguish these types of words from coordinating conjunctions (cc). For simplicity's sake, students can mark these clause starters with a *cl*.

The main difference is that when coordinating conjunctions (*for, and, nor, but, or, yet,* and *so*) are added to a main clause, we still have a main clause. When subordinating conjunctions (*when, while, where,* etc.) are added to a main clause, they turn it into a dependent clause. The punctuation changes too. See under Stylistic Techniques: Dress-ups: Clause Starters, page G-38; and Sentence Openers: #5 Clausal Opener, page G-42.

Advanced: Confusingly, *since, until,* and *as* sometimes function as prepositions, and *because of* is also a preposition. See tips for distinguishing them under Stylistic Techniques: Sentence Openers: #5 Clausal Opener, page G-42.

Advanced: Also confusingly, *as, where, when, while* and *whereas* sometimes start adjective clauses or function as coordinating conjunctions. See Sentences, Clauses, and Phrases: Clauses: Dependent Clauses (Advanced), page G-17; and Stylistic Techniques: Sentence Openers: #5 Clausal Opener, page G-42.

Conjunctive Adverbs (Advanced)

These words are a writer's plague—albeit an important group of words!—because they are often confused with subordinating conjunctions but need different punctuation.

Some common conjunctive adverbs: *however, therefore, then, moreover, consequently, otherwise, nevertheless, thus, furthermore, instead, otherwise.*

Learn this principle: When you add a conjunctive adverb to a main clause, it is still a main clause, which is not the case with subordinating conjunctions.

How this matters:

1. If conjunctive adverbs start a sentence, usually follow them with a comma as you would any transitional word or expression. The exception is short conjunctive adverbs like *then,* which do not require a pause.

> Examples: **Then** *they dropped it when we were older.* **Moreover,** *didn't they realize cell phones were for emergencies only?*

2. If a conjunctive adverb falls between two main clauses that belong together in one sentence, put a semicolon before it and comma after: **MC; ca, MC.**

> Example: *Years of indulgence had spoiled her beyond recognition;* **however,** *Lady Constance recalled a time in Dorinda's childhood when she had been a lovable child.*

> If the main clauses express two different ideas, separate them with a period.

The lady bent down and awarded Gawain a kiss. **Then** *she appealed to him to rhapsodize about the tribulations and treasures of true love.*

3. If conjunctive adverbs fall in the middle of a sentence, however, use two commas or none, depending on whether you need a clear pause around them.

Examples: *Chanticleer ignored her advice,* **however.** *Pertelote* **therefore** *argued more vehemently for laxatives from the garden. Chanticleer* **then** *countered with another round of dire dreams, which* **nevertheless** *failed to convince Pertelote.*

Interjections

Interjections are words that express a strong emotion, such as *ow, oh, ugh, whew*. They usually are set off with commas, but if they have a strong exclamatory message, you may put an exclamation mark after them. Alone, they do not count as a sentence.

"Oops! I do believe I've broken your leg."

"Oh, yes, benevolent frog!"

"Yuck! I won't touch another bite!"

Sentences, Clauses, and Phrases

Sentences

A sentence expresses one complete thought. To do so, it must have at least one main clause.

Sentence sense. Writers often string together more than one main clause in a sentence, often with the coordinating conjunction *and*, when those main clauses would be more powerful as separate sentences. When students are ready to understand the concept, discourage this practice.

Sentence fragments. A fragment is an error in which a sentence has phrases and/or dependent clauses but no main clause.

Servants came forth, attending to his horse. Welcoming the warrior. The second part is an unacceptable fragment.

In fiction and even in academic writing for some teachers, fragments that do not leave the reader hanging and that fit the flow of the paragraph are dramatic and effective. *Fix It!* stories permit such fragments, especially in dialogue when complete sentences would sound unnatural. The key is whether or not the fragment leaves the reader feeling as if something more is needed.

"Would you like me to rescue your ball?"

"Oh, yes!" (acceptable fragment)

Because students often use fragments ineffectively in formal writing, many teachers forbid the use of any fragment. Discuss which fragments in the *Fix It!* stories work well and which ones do not in order to arm students with the practice of recognizing sentence fragments. This will also help them distinguish phrases and dependent clauses from main, or independent, clauses.

Clauses and Phrases

Failure to recognize the basic clauses and phrases that form the underlying structure of sentences is at the heart of most students' inability to punctuate their sentences properly.

When older students struggle with knowing where to place their commas, this, along with knowing basic parts of speech, is most likely the root problem. They cannot recognize a main clause if they do not know what a subject-verb pair is, and they cannot know this if they do not distinguish nouns, pronouns, and verbs from other parts of speech.

The different levels of *Fix It!* teach grammar progressively in this way: beginning with basic parts of speech, then identifying phrases and clauses, and gradually adding in punctuation. Once students understand the basic structure of their sentences, they will know how to apply the punctuation rules.

Phrases

A phrase is a group of related words that does not have both a subject and a verb.

Prepositional phrases. Practically speaking, these are the only phrases worth teaching. Finding prepositional phrases helps get the "noise" out of the sentence and makes it easier for students to see their clauses. It also helps them properly identify #2 sentence openers. See Parts of Speech: Prepositions, page G-11; and Stylistic Techniques: Sentence Openers: #2 Prepositional Opener, page G-39.

Appositive. A convenient word for a simple concept, an appositive is a noun that renames the noun that comes right before it. Example: *Robin Hood,* **the archer***.* The only reason appositives are worth flagging is that they usually are set off with commas but sometimes not. See under Punctuation: Commas: Rule 15: Essential-Nonessential Elements, page G-24.

Clauses

A clause is a group of related words that must have both a subject and a verb.

Main Clauses (MC)

These are clauses that can stand alone as a sentence.

a. *Main clause* is abbreviated *MC* in *Fix It!* The MC is also known as an independent clause or strong clause.

b. MCs usually start with a subject or with an article (*a, an, the*) and/or adjectives plus subject. Example: *The poor soldiers returned* follows the pattern of "Article (*The*) adjective (*poor*) subject (*soldiers*) verb (*returned*)."

Sometimes the subject-verb will be inverted, with the verb coming before the subject. Examples: *There gathered around him displaced countrymen.* subject-verb = countrymen gathered. *Up rose his Merry Men.* subject-verb = Merry Men are. These are still MCs.

c. When identifying MCs, include prepositional phrases in the middle or at the end of the clause but not ones that come before MCs. Follow common sense in determining which words must group with the basic subject and verb of the main clause.

d. Sometimes dependent clauses (like *who-which*'s) are included in a MC and needed for it to make sense. Example: *I have never met a man who could topple me off a bridge.* The MC includes the dependent who clause and does not makes sense as just *I have never met a man.*

Dependent Clauses (DC)

These are clauses that cannot stand alone as a sentence.

a. *Dependent clause* is abbreviated *DC* in *Fix It!* It is also known as a subordinate clause or weak clause.

b. DCs are basically main clauses with another word or words in front that turn the main clause into something that leaves us hanging, that cannot stand alone as a sentence.

For practical purposes, it is enough for younger students to recognize the dependent clause starters *who, which, that,* and the subordinating conjunctions, the www.asia. buwu words *when, while, where, as, since, if, although, because, until, whereas, unless.*

As an example, start with a main clause: *The foresters discovered them in the act.* Now add a www word: *Although the foresters discovered them in the act.* There is still a subject and verb, so this is a clause and not a phrase. However, the second version leaves us hanging. *Although this is true, something else must also be true.*

DCs (Dependent Clauses) must be attached to a MC (Main Clause) to be a legal sentence.

c. To simplify grammar, focus on teaching just two types of DCs: 1. *who-which* clauses, and 2. www.asia.b clauses. In *Fix It!* adverb clauses that begin with one of the www words are abbreviated as *AC.*

See Stylistic Techniques: Dress-Ups: *Who-Which* Clause, page G-36, and Clause Starters (www.asia.b), page G-38; and Stylistic Techniques: Sentence Openers: #5 Clausal Opener, page G-42.

Dependent Clauses (Advanced)

Understanding DCs well and punctuating them perfectly every time can get complex. The amount of time it would take to teach most students these finer points of grammar is not always worth it, but it may help teachers to understand the following.

Dependent clauses function in different ways, which can affect their punctuation.

1. Adverb clauses, a.k.a. adverbial clauses (AC)

Most of the time, a clause starter from the www word list will start an adverb clause. It should not be set off with a comma if it falls in the middle or at the end of a sentence (**MC AC**), but it takes a comma after the clause if it is an opener (**AC, MC**).

2. Adjective clauses

This usually starts with a relative pronoun, mainly *who, which,* or *that.* Adjective clauses usually follow nouns or pronouns and describe the nouns they follow: *the **arrow that** Robin shot...; the **princess, who** was artful and cunning....*

Adjective clauses are set off with commas if they are nonessential to the rest of the sentence but not set off with commas if they are essential. See under Punctuation: Commas: Rule 15: Essential-Nonessential Elements, page G-24.

Unfortunately—and this is one of the areas where grammar gets messy—three of the subordinating conjunctions that are in the clause starter list, *as, where,* and *when,* sometimes start adjective clauses and thus act as relative pronouns. This matters because adverb clauses in the middle or end of sentences never take commas, but adjective clauses take commas when they are nonessential.

Contrast these examples:

*The roof is formed of shells, which open and close **as** the water flows over them.* *As* is a subordinating conjunction meaning *while;* it starts an adverb clause, so no comma.

*The outcome of joy is invariably woe, **as** all creatures know. As* is a relative pronoun meaning *a fact that;* it starts a nonessential clause and needs a comma.

Tip: Conjunctive adverbs like *however, therefore, then* and coordinating conjunctions like *and, or, but* do not turn a MC into a DC.

Other messy exceptions are *while* and *whereas*, which can be subordinating conjunctions (no comma before them) or coordinating conjunctions (comma before them when they join main clauses).

Contrast these sentences:

> *The second soldier took the road to the right **while** he thought about his next plan of action.* No comma because *while* is a subordinating conjunction starting an adverb clause, and adverb clause dress-ups are not set off with commas. *While* means "at the same time that" here.

> *The second soldier took the path to the right, **while** the other two determined to travel down the road to the left.* Comma because *while* is a coordinating conjunction joining two main clauses (**MC, cc MC**). As a cc, *while* and *whereas* convey a contrast.

3. Noun clauses

These function as nouns. Most often, they follow a verb and begin with *that*, one of the words that confusingly can also begin an adjective clause. You can tell the difference because *that* adjective clauses follow a noun while *that* noun clauses follow a verb. Example: *People felt that Robin Hood was like them. That* follows the verb *felt* so starts a noun clause.

Tip: A clause is a noun clause if you can substitute a pronoun for it. Example: *People felt **that** Robin Hood was like them. People felt **it**.* Makes sense! But: *Robin returned to the town **that** he had left. Robin returned to the town **it**?* This does not make sense, so this *that* starts an adjective, not a noun, clause.

Where grammar gets even muddier is that *when, where, who* and other words sometimes start noun clauses. However, students will not run into these situations enough in marking dress-ups and openers to make it worth spending the time to teach noun clauses. Fortunately, students rarely have trouble punctuating noun clauses, so learning about them becomes a moot issue.

Punctuation

End Marks . ? !

A sentence may end with a **period**, **question mark**, or **exclamation mark**.

Do not double punctuate. Not *"You're sure?!"* or *"Hah!," he said.* But *"You're sure?"* and *"Hah!" he said.*

Rule 1. Use periods at the end of statements and in abbreviations.

He bowed and walked away.

Advanced: Comma splices and **fused sentences** occur when students join main clauses with only commas or with no punctuation. MCs need something stronger to hold them together, often a period. See under Semicolons, page G-26.

Rule 2. Periods (and commas) go inside closing quotation marks.

"The better man should cross first."

Rule 3. Use question marks after direct questions.

Did you ever hear the story of the three poor soldiers?

Rule 4. Use exclamation marks when the statement expresses strong emotion, but do not overuse them. When a character is said to exclaim something, the context begs for an exclamation mark.

"No one calls me a coward!"

"Hah!" the other exclaimed.

Quotations " "

Rule 1. Use quotation marks to enclose direct quotations but not indirect speech, which usually begins with *that*. Quotation marks should "hug" the words they enclose—that is, there should not be a space between the quotation mark and the word or punctuation it encloses.

"It's no wonder that child has turned out so blemished," clucked Lady Constance. (direct)

Secretly he thought that in beauty she surpassed Queen Guinevere herself. (indirect)

Rule 2. The attribution is the narrative that sets up a quotation with a speaking verb (*he said*). Set attributions off from quotations with commas. The attribution can come before, after, or in the middle of the quotation.

When using your computer, be sure you are creating *curly quotes* (" ") and not *straight quotes* (" ").

Straight quotes should be reserved for measurements, and only when the format is very tight, such as 6" 2' for six feet, two inches.

Patterns: **speaking verb, "quote"** or **"quote," speaking verb**

> He *answered*, "Hand me a stout bow and straight arrow."

> "I will join your band," *announced* the stranger.

> "You stand back," *responded* his adversary, "since I am the better man."

Rule 3. Commas and periods always go inside closing quotations (unless they are followed by parentheses, in which case they go after the parentheses).

> "It's gold, you know."

Rule 4. Exclamation marks and question marks go inside closing quotations when they are part of the material quoted; otherwise, they go outside. Also, use only one ending mark of punctuation—the stronger—with quotation marks, em dashes excepted.

> "If only I could have my ball back, I would bestow a handsome reward on my benefactor!"

> "Dorinda, who was at the door?" King Morton inquired.

Rule 5. If a quotation ends in an exclamation mark or question but is followed by an attribution, use a lowercase letter at the beginning of the attribution (unless it starts with a proper noun) because the attribution is part of the same sentence as the quotation.

> "Have at him!" cried Will Stutely.

Rule 6. When a spoken sentence is interrupted, close the first part and begin the second with quotation marks. Do not capitalize the first letter of the continuation.

> "By the great yew bow of Saint Withold," cried the stranger, "that is a shot indeed!"

Rule 7. When typing, place thoughts in italics instead of in quotation marks.

> *It's time she was humbled a little*, thought the wise soldier.

When handwriting, use quotation marks.

Rule 8. Use italics or place quotation marks around words referred to as words. Trick: Insert "the word(s)" or "the name" before the word in question to tell if this rule applies.

> Since "Little" is indeed your true name.... (Since the name "Little"...)

> He would have none of this recent drivel of dropping "sir" and "madam" when addressing one's elders. (dropping the words "sir" and "madam")

Rule 9. Use single quotation marks for quotations within quotations. This is the only time to use single quotations.

> "She also insisted on stripping the top coverlets from all the mattresses because, as she put it, 'They might be unclean.'"

Rule 10. In conversation, if someone is speaking and changes topic, start a new paragraph. However, close his first paragraph without a quotation mark and open his new paragraph with a quotation mark.

The missing quotation mark at the end of the first paragraph signals that he has not finished speaking. The opening quotation mark in the next paragraph reminds us that someone is still speaking.

> Robin accepted the challenge. "I will stoop to you as I never stooped to man before.

> ¶ "Friend Stutely, cut down a white piece of bark four fingers tall and wide."

Apostrophes '

Rule 1. Use an apostrophe with contractions, placing it where the letter(s) have been removed. Note that in formal writing contractions should be avoided, but they are acceptable in fiction, especially in dialogue.

"I'll figure out how to trick them."

"It's too bad, but we'd better go our separate ways."

Rule 2. Use an apostrophe to show possession. To form plural possessives, make the noun plural first; then add an apostrophe. An exception is irregular plural possessives like *children's* and *women's*.

the second soldier's turn

the soldiers' last night at the palace (the last night of all three soldiers)

Rule 3. Never use an apostrophe with possessive pronouns (*his, hers, its, theirs, ours, yours*) since they already show possession. Teach students the differences in these tricky pairs:

Possessive Pronoun	Contraction
its	it's (it is; remember by it's)
whose	who's (who is)
theirs	there's (there is)

Just like with quotation marks, when using your computer, be sure you are using *curly apostrophes* (') and not *straight apostrophes* (').

Commas ,

Rule 1. Adjectives before a noun

Use commas to separate two or more coordinate adjectives before a noun. **Coordinate adjectives** each independently describe the noun, as in *dewy, silent leaves*.

Do not use commas to separate **cumulative adjectives**, in which the first adjective modifies both the second adjective and the noun, as in *one fair morning*. The adjectives are cumulative if the last one deals with time, age, or color *or* if it forms a compound noun with the noun (*apple tree*).

Two tricks help distinguish coordinate from cumulative, but these are just tricks that depend on a quick response, not rules. If you think about it too long, it is harder to tell.

Adjectives are coordinate and need a comma if you can

1. reverse their order.

2. add *and* between them.

Examples: With *pointed, protruding nose*, it sounds right to say both *protruding, pointed nose* and *pointed and protruding nose*, so the adjectives are coordinate and the comma is necessary.

With *stout oak staff*, it sounds awkward to say either *oak stout staff* or *stout and oak staff*, so the adjectives are cumulative and should not have a comma.

Occasionally students will put a comma between an adjective and the noun it modifies, as in *the pointed, protruding, nose*. Be on the lookout for this and squash this habit if it forms!

Rule 2. Quotations

Use a comma with a verb of speaking that introduces a direct quotation, whether the verb comes before or after the quotation.

Older students who do not correctly punctuate their sentences rarely learn by memorizing punctuation rules. The problem goes back to understanding the underlying sentence structure. See under Sentences, Clauses, and Phrases: Clauses and Phrases, page G-15.

Students with weak understanding of when to punctuate should start with the first story of *Fix It!*

"King Mel loathes courtly balls," Lord Ashton *protested*.

Lord Ashton *protested*, "King Mel loathes courtly balls."

Rule 3. Nouns of Direct Address (NDAs)

Set off nouns of direct address (NDAs) with commas.

"*Fool*, you have killed the king's deer."

"For fourteen days we have enjoyed no sport, *my friends*."

Rule 4. Items in a series

Pattern: a, b, and c. Use commas to separate three or more items in a series. These items must be the same part of speech or same grammatical construction, such as phrases or clauses. The last two items are usually connected by a coordinating conjunction.

Robin was *mature, strong*, and *dauntless*. (three adjectives)

He *accepted* the match, *grabbed* his bow and arrow, and *started* off from Locksley. (three verbs)

The Oxford comma. Current trend is to keep the Oxford comma, which is the comma before the coordinating conjunction in three or more items in a series. Although the Oxford comma is optional if there is no danger of misreading, writers do not always recognize potential confusion. It is never wrong to include the Oxford comma, so it is easier to include it always.

Example: *To his hens, Chanticleer gave fine gifts, the pleasure of his singing and corn.* Ambiguity: Are "the pleasure of his singing and corn" the actual gifts, or are these three separate items? The Oxford comma clarifies that these are three separate items: *Chanticleer gave fine gifts, the pleasure of his singing, and corn.*

Pattern: a and b. Do not use commas with only two items in a series unless those items are main clauses.

You shall enjoy succulent *venison* and the stoutest tasting *ale*. (two nouns)

He will receive a *trouncing* and a *ducking* himself. (two -ing words)

Rule 5. Compound verb. Pattern: MC cc 2nd verb.

Do not use a comma before a coordinating conjunction that joins two verbs (a compound verb) with the same subject. It helps to think of this as joining only two items (two verbs) in a series. You will not see a second subject after the coordinating conjunction.

They *built* great fires and *roasted* the does. (two verbs)

He also *had* the little man in the red jacket for his guest and *treated* him graciously.

Rule 6. Main clauses with a coordinating conjunction. Pattern: MC, cc MC

Use a comma before a coordinating conjunction that joins two main clauses. You will see a subject and verb after the coordinating conjunction.

"*He is* of diminished princely stature, *and he doesn't care* for polo."

They had fought well in the wars, *but* now *they were* out of work and destitute.

Rule 7. Introductory prepositional phrases (#2 sentence openers)

Use commas after introductory prepositional phrases of five or more words. The comma is optional with fewer than five words. With short prepositional openers, let the pause test be your guide: If it sounds better with a pause, include a comma; if it does not need a pause, leave it out.

For advanced writers, emphasize that this is the only situation when quotations are set up with a comma. In research, quotations are often worked into the text with no punctuation or with a colon when they follow a main clause that they also illustrate.

Technically, the comma in the MC, cc MC pattern is optional when the clauses are short and there is no danger of misreading.

However, since it can cause confusion to omit it, it is easier to include it always.

On his journey north Gawain encountered few obstacles. (comma optional)

From stone *to* stone they cavorted about. (comma optional)

"*By* the faith *of* my heart, never have I been called a craven in all my life!"

With a string of opening introductory prepositional phrases, save the comma for the end of all of them, even if one of them is long.

Not: During the long and arduous weeks, of preparation, for the ball, Mel was shuffled off to the hunting lodge.

But: During the long and arduous weeks of preparation for the ball, Mel was shuffled off to the hunting lodge.

Advanced: When the introductory prepositional phrase is followed by a verb instead of noun or pronoun, do not add the comma.

Behind them close on their heels *bounded* the cow and the calf.

Rule 8. Mid-sentence prepositional phrases

Prepositional phrases in the middle of sentences are not set off with commas.

The stranger shot *at the small white square* fixed to its front.

Rule 9. Transitional expressions and interjections

Use a comma after introductory transitional expressions and interjections. Usually include commas on both sides of interrupting words or phrases that appear elsewhere in a sentence.

Meanwhile, Robin's men lay off to the side of the prodigious oak.

Moreover, didn't they realize cell phones were intended for emergencies only?

The palace accountant ordered them a new HDTV, complete with a surround system, *too*.

As grown-up girls, *however*, they could go when they pleased.

When an interjection expresses a strong emotion, use an exclamation mark instead.

Alas! In an ox's stall this night I shall be murdered where I lie.

Rule 10. Introductory adverb clauses (#5 sentence openers). Pattern: AC, MC

Use commas after introductory #5 adverb clause sentence openers, even if they are short. An adverb clause is a type of dependent clause. See Stylistic Techniques: Sentence Openers: #5 Clausal Opener, page G-42.

Although the foresters discovered them in the act, they narrowly escaped.

Since the problem was obvious, he continued after a pause.

When he finished, they thanked their old friend heartily for his kindness.

Because the Sheriff of Nottingham was related to the slain forester, he had a vendetta to catch Robin Hood.

Rule 11. Adverb clause dress-up. Pattern: MC AC

Do not use a comma with mid-sentence adverb clauses. See Stylistic Techniques: Dress-Ups: www.asia.b words, page G-38. See exceptions in Rules 13 and 15 below.

Robin observed him *as* he trimmed his staff.

"Remain on the other side *while* I quickly make a staff."

"I will tan your hide *until* it's as many colors as a beggar's cloak *if* you touch your bow."

Rule 12. Comparisons.

Do not use a comma to separate parts of a comparison.

O disconsolate hens, louder was your keening *than* that of senators' wives in Rome.

Rule 13. Contrasting elements.

Use commas to separate contrasting parts of a sentence.

The ideas in this story are the cock's thoughts, not mine.

This is especially confusing with the www words *although, while,* and *whereas.* When they contrast the main clause before them, set them off with a comma, despite the more common rule **MC AC.**

"Now you flinch for fear, *although* you have felt no harm."

"Whatever I win in the woods I will award you in the evening, *while* all that you have gained you must bestow on me."

This sometimes applies to the cc *but* when it presents a strong contrast, even when it is joining only two items in a series that are not main clauses and therefore normally do not take a comma.

"Dreams are often a portent not just of joy, *but* of tribulations to come."

Rule 14. Participial Phrases (#4 sentence openers)

Use commas after introductory -ing participial phrases, even if they are short.

Excusing herself from the table, Dorinda hastened away.

Participial phrases in the middle or at the end of sentences are usually nonessential and therefore set off with commas.

Her sisters rose from the depths, *singing plaintively.*

Rule 15. Essential-Nonessential elements (a.k.a. restrictive-nonrestrictive)

Set off *who-which* clauses, appositives, participial phrases, and adjective clauses with commas if they are nonessential. Do not put commas around them if they are essential.

If the clause or phrase is necessary to the meaning of the rest of the sentence or if it specifies which one of something is being discussed, it is essential and should not be enclosed in commas.

If it does not alter the meaning of the rest of the sentence or if the person or thing is adequately identified, it is nonessential and needs commas, even though it may be adding important information. *Nonessential* should not be taken to mean unimportant.

Tricks to test:

1. Mentally remove the clause or phrase from the sentence to see if it alters the information in the rest of the sentence or specifies who or what is meant. If it does not, the element is nonessential and should be set off with commas.

2. Put parentheses around the clause or phrase. If the sentence still seems to work, the clause or phrase is probably nonessential.

Importantly, often whether or not you use commas changes the meaning. For example, it is correct to punctuate the following who clause as essential or nonessential: *Even the footmen, who once toadied to her, snubbed her.* With commas, it is saying that all footmen

Tip: Sometimes it is not crystal clear whether a clause or phrase is essential or nonessential. Ask these questions:

Does it affect the meaning of the rest of the sentence?

Does it specify which particular noun is intended?

Then use your best guess. Grammarians will not always agree on particular examples!

Tip: The concept of essential and nonessential elements does not apply to sentence openers, which have separate rules of punctuation. Test this out only on phrases and clauses in the middle or at the end of sentences.

snubbed her, and, incidentally, all once toadied to her. Without commas it is saying that only those footmen who used to toady to her now snubbed her: *Even the footmen who once toadied to her snubbed her.*

Examples:

"Be ready to heed my call, *which will sound as three short blasts upon the bugle horn.*" (nonessential which clause)

> If we remove the which clause from the sentence, the main clause meaning does not change: the speaker still wants them to be ready to heed his call. The which clause is therefore nonessential, even though it adds important information, and should be set off with commas.

Tip: The word *that* can replace *which* in essential clauses.

He had shot a deer *that the king reserved for his own table.* (essential that clause, so no comma)

> This clause is essential because it specifies which particular deer. He did not shoot just any deer but one reserved for the king.

"It was agreed that the poor soldier *who had already suffered from the power of the apple* should undertake the task." (essential who clause)

> The who clause specifies which soldier—the one who had already suffered from the apple's power—so is needed in the sentence and therefore not set off with commas. It restricts the information to that particular soldier, which is why these are sometimes called restrictive clauses.

She had confessed the truth to Lady Constance, *who now played her trump card.* (nonessential who clause)

> Lady Constance is already sufficiently identified. The who clause adds an important detail but does not alter the meaning of the rest of the sentence so is nonessential and needs a comma.

the archer *Robin Hood* (essential appositive)

> Without his name, we would not know which archer is intended, so this is an essential appositive and should not be set off with a comma.

Robin Hood, *the archer* (nonessential appositive)

> It adds information but does not restrict the information to a particular Robin Hood or change the meaning of the rest of the sentence.

Robin Hood rose, *needing a change.* (nonessential participial phrase)

> He still rose, regardless of whether or not he needed a change. The participial phrase adds information but does not alter the meaning of the main clause.

Tip: Most participial phrases are nonessential.

Advanced: Sometimes *when, as,* and *where* start adjective clauses instead of adverb clauses. When they do, they can be essential or nonessential. This next example illustrates a nonessential adjective clause (*where*) and a nonessential participial phrase (*frightened*).

> Robin waded to the bank, *where* the little fish scattered and fled, *frightened* at his splashing.

Semicolons ;

Rule 1. Use semicolons to join main clauses when they are so intricately linked they belong in the same sentence. Otherwise, use a period. Pattern: **MC; MC**

"He sounds like just my type; he sounds just like me!"

Advanced: Conjunctive adverbs (words like *therefore, however, nevertheless, moreover, furthermore*) do not turn a main clause into a dependent one; therefore, use a semicolon before the conjunctive adverb if it joins two main clauses that belong in one sentence. Use a period if the main clauses should be two sentences.

Run-ons. A **comma splice** is the error caused by joining two main clauses with only a comma when they need to be joined with something stronger, such as a semicolon, a period, or a comma plus a coordinating conjunction. A **fused sentence** is the error of joining two main clauses with no punctuation or coordinating conjunction.

Comma splice: *Gawain glanced up, the great ax descended.* Something stronger than a comma is needed to join these two main clauses.

There are four common solutions to run-ons, which work better or worse depending on the sentence:

1. Period: Gawain glanced up. The great ax descended.

2. Semicolon: Gawain glanced up; the great ax descended.

> **a.** Use a semicolon only when the two clauses are so inextricably linked (and often parallel in construction) that they are expressing one idea and need to go together in one sentence.

> **b.** A semicolon is more effective than a period here because it shows there is a link between these two ideas, but solutions 3 and 4 are better still.

3. Comma + cc: Gawain glanced up, *and* the great ax descended.

4. Adverb clause: Subordinate one of the clauses by starting it with one of the www.asia.b words:

> **a.** As Gawain glanced up, the great ax descended. (Comma needed after the introductory adverb clause: **AC, MC**.)

> **b.** Gawain glanced up as the great ax descended. (No comma needed with adverb clause dress-up: **MC AC**.)

> This is the best solution to this comma splice because the subordinating conjunction *as* explains how the two clauses are related: Gawain happened to glance up at the same time that the Green Knight lowered his ax.

A period is usually the easiest and often the best solution for run-ons, especially for younger students.

Advanced: Rule 2. Use semicolons to separate items in a series when the items contain internal commas. (Rare)

Highborn women lamented when Troy, that noble city celebrated by Homer, fell through trickery; when Pyrrhus, ancient Greek ruler, seized King Priam by the beard; and when the Romans, ruthless and crazed, torched Carthage to the ground.

Colons :

Rule 1. Use a colon after a main clause to introduce an explanation or a list when a phrase like *for example* or *that is* is not included. Lists take no punctuation if there is not a main clause setting them up.

"Yet one other boon I ask: please accept this simple souvenir from me."

Advanced: High school students will benefit from this pattern when they make a point and want to use a quotation to support that point. The colon is the perfect mark of punctuation to join the main clause to the quotation that illustrates it. Think of colons as meaning *see what follows* or *an example follows*.

Rule 2. In business or technical writing, use colons after subheads or words like *example* to set up what follows. Rarely use this in academic papers.

To: Example:
Fix: Dear Sir or Madam:

Rule 3. Use a colon to separate the hour and minutes when specifying time of day.

"We have a manicure scheduled for 10:15."

Hyphens -

Rule 1. Use hyphens in some compound nouns, such as *lady-in-waiting*. Consult a dictionary to check whether the compound noun should be written as one word (*marksman*), two words (*apple tree*), or hyphenated words.

Rule 2. Use hyphens with compound adjectives in front of a noun but usually not after a noun: jewel-encrusted crown, nineteenth-century author, well-attired people. Her crown was jewel encrusted. He lived in the nineteenth century. The people were well attired.

Rule 3. Use hyphens with compound numbers from *twenty-one* to *ninety-nine* and with spelled out fractions like *one-fourth*.

Rule 4. Use hyphens in phone numbers: 555-1212.

Em Dashes and Parentheses — ( )

Although em dashes and parentheses should be used sparingly, especially in academic writing, they can be effective tools when used properly. Distinguish between the **hyphen** (-), which joins things like compound words, and the **em dash**, which is longer (—).

Rule 1. Use em dashes in place of commas when you want to emphasize or draw attention to something. Use **parentheses** in place of commas to minimize the importance of something or to offer an aside. Em dashes are loud, parentheses quiet.

Chanticleer would raise his beak high on a fine summer evening and sing—to the jealousy of neighboring roosters for miles around—such ecstasy had he in his crowing.

(Notice that in fairy tales, characters don't have great curiosity about such oddities as talking frogs.)

Rule 2. Use em dashes to indicate an interruption in speech or a sudden break in thought.

His younger daughter—now there was another topic that brought red to his face.

Rule 3. Use em dashes to set off nonessential elements that have commas inside them.

The poor widow owned a few farm animals—three hefty sows, three cows, and a sheep dubbed Molly—with which she attempted to eke out a living.

Rule 4. Use parentheses for area codes in phone numbers: (260) 555-1212.

Pattern: **MC: illustrating list, example, or quotation.**

Remember, a main clause must come before a colon.

Advanced: When a main clause follows the colon, use a capital letter under two circumstances:

1) The colon introduces more than one sentence (rare).

2) It introduces a formal statement or quotation.

Example:
Charlemagne stated the dual boon of herbs: "An herb is the friend of physicians and the praise of cooks."

Em dashes get their name from the fact that they are roughly the width of the upper-case M in the alphabet.

There is no key for a em dash on your keyboard, but there are shortcuts:

On a PC, type **ctrl-alt-minus sign:** specifically, the minus sign on the numeric keypad on the far right of the keyboard.

On a Mac, type **option-shift-hyphen.**

Ellipsis Points ...

Rule 1. Use ellipsis points to signal hesitation or a reflective pause, especially in dialogue in fiction. Rarely use them in formal papers for this reason.

"Ahem..." Lord Ashton cleared his throat conspicuously.

"Um... certainly... the mattress test."

Rule 2. In composition or academic writing, use three spaced periods (the ellipsis mark) to indicate an omission in a quotation. It is not necessary to use the ellipsis mark at the beginning or end of an excerpted passage.

Rule 3. In quoting another source, if the part you leave out spans more than one sentence, use four ellipsis points. The fourth one is actually a period.

Additional Rules and Concepts

Indentation Rules

Indent at the beginning of appropriate sentences to start new paragraphs. On the student pages, mark sentences that need indenting with the editing notation for a paragraph, which looks like a backwards P: ¶.

In copy work, indent by doing two things: 1. start on the next line, and 2. start writing ½ inch from the left margin.

Begin a new paragraph with the following:

1. A new speaker.

    a. Start the paragraph at the beginning of the sentence in which someone is speaking, even if the quotation appears later in the sentence. Example: *She cried out with great force, "Thieves!"*

    b. If a narrative sentence sets up the quotation, it can go in the same paragraph as the quoted sentence. Example: *The stranger came right to the point. "It is cowardly to stand there with a lethal arrow aimed at my heart."*

    c. If narrative follows a quotation in a separate sentence but points directly back to the quotation, it can also go in the same paragraph. Example: *"It is cowardly to stand there with a lethal arrow aimed at my heart." The stranger did not mince words.*

2. A new topic.

    a. This is the fuzziest to determine. Generally, if the narrator or a character switches topic or the focus, start a new paragraph.

    b. The problem is that topics are a bit like a camera lens: they can sweep a broad scene or zoom in on details. If not much time is devoted to any of the details, you can safely combine different but related points in one paragraph, just as a photograph of the ocean—which takes in the water, sky, beach, swimmers, and even distant ships—can be as harmonious as one of a single shell on shore.

3. A new place.

    a. Start a new paragraph when the story switches to a new scene.

    b. If several switches are made in quick succession, such as a character's journey to find something, it may be less choppy to keep in one paragraph. Encourage older students to be flexible in making these choices, but if students are more comfortable with a stricter interpretation (hence more paragraphs), that is fine.

You may have noticed that this book does not follow this indentation format. These rules are perfect for students, though, because they typically do not have the typographic tools that book designers have, such as being able to control the space between paragraphs.

4. A new time.

    a. Same principles as with place: start a new paragraph with a new time unless there are several time shifts in close succession that make sense together in a single paragraph.

The rules for new paragraphs in fiction are less rigid than they are in academic writing. Do not get hung up on the details, but try to follow the main principles and aim for some consistency. If students make a reasonable case based on these principles for something other than what the book suggests, let them choose. In practice, paragraph divisions are clearer and more critical in academic writing, so we can be more flexible with fiction.

Capitalization Rules

Rule 1. Capitalize the first word of a sentence and of a quoted sentence, even when it does not begin the full sentence.

    The stranger responded, "You joke like a numbskull!"

Rule 2. Use lowercase to continue interrupted quotations.

    "Princess," he began, "you have a visitor at the door."

Rule 3. Capitalize proper nouns and words derived from proper nouns.

    Sherwood Forest; Robin Hood; Arthurian; Spartan

Rule 4. Capitalize people's titles when used with a name or as a substitute for a name in a noun of direct address. Do not capitalize titles when used without a name. Do not capitalize family members unless used as a substitute for a name or with a name.

    The Sheriff of Nottingham was related to the forester whom Robin Hood killed.

    The sheriff was related to the forester whom Robin Hood killed.

    "Can you clean the bullet from his wound, Doctor?"

    He succeeded his father as king.

> An exception to Rule 4 is *sir* or *madam* as a noun of direct address: *"Stand back, sir,"* demanded Robin.

Rule 5. Capitalize calendar names (days of the week and months) but not seasons.

    the month of June; in the spring; on Wednesday

Rule 6. Capitalize compass directions only when they refer to specific geographic regions, such as the South, or are part of a proper noun, such as North Carolina or New South Wales.

    On his journey north Gawain encountered few obstacles. (He is heading in a northward direction but not traveling to a region known as the North.)

Rule 7. Capitalize the first and last words of titles and subtitles and all other words except articles, coordinating conjunctions, and prepositions.

    A shy, small girl recited "Mary Had a Little Lamb."

    Your Knights of the Round Table are reputed superior in courtesy and arms.

    Note: Titles of long works like books, magazines, and movies should be italicized. Titles of short works like poems, short stories, and articles in magazines should be in quotation marks.

> When writing longhand, it is customary to underline words that you will want to italicize.

Numbers Rules

Different style guides give different rules about how to write numbers. These simplified rules follow the principles of the Chicago Manual of Style.

Rule 1. Spell out numbers that can be expressed in one or two words; use figures for other numbers.

> The younger of his two daughters had racked up one thousand text messages on her cell phone in a single month!

Rule 2. Spell out ordinal numbers.

> In another year the second sister was permitted to rise to the surface.

Rule 3. Use numerals with dates..

> Exiting the hall, the stranger called back, "Meet me at the Green Chapel in one year and one day on January 1, 1400."

Rule 4. When numbers are mixed with symbols, use figures.

> "We can expect at least 40% of those invited to attend, or 238 guests."

Homophones and Usage

Homophones are words that sound alike but are spelled differently and have different meanings. Usage errors occur when students use one word when another is meant, often with words that are spelled similarly.

Encourage students to start a list of troublesome words to consult whenever they write.

Some common errors:

1. *there, their, they're; your, you're*

> **a.** *There* is the adverb pointing to a place or point: *over there; there is the spot.*

> **b.** *Their* and *your* are possessive pronouns: *their journey; your weapon.*

> **c.** *They're* and *you're* are contractions meanings *they are* and *you are*: *they're finished; you're spying.*

2. *to, two, too*

> **a.** *To* is the preposition: *to the soldiers' aid; to the right. To* is also used in infinitives, the "to + verb" form of a verb: *to rush; to seize.*

> **b.** *Two* is the number.

> **c.** *Too* means either *also* or *to an excessive degree* or *too much.* It is easy to remember because it has one too many o's!

3. *its, it's*

> **a.** *Its* is the possessive: *its bark* (the bark of the tree).

> **b.** *It's* is the contraction *it is: It's too bad.* Teach the difference by explaining that the apostrophe in *it's* is like a little *i: it's.*

> **c.** *Its'* is always incorrect.

4. *then, than*

> Use *then* to mean *next* or *immediately afterward.* Use *than* for a comparison. *After Alice drank the potion, she was then shorter than she was a moment before.*

5. *lie, lay*

    a. Simplify this problem pair by explaining that someone lies himself down but lays down an object.

    b. The three main verb forms:

        i. to lie: *lie, lay, lain* (present, past, past participle)

        ii. to lay: *lay, laid, laid*

    One reason students have trouble with these words is that the past tense of *to lie* is the same as the present tense of *to lay*.

    c. For some students, memorizing a simple sentence can help with the confusing past tense forms: *Henny Hen lay down* (something she did to herself) *after she laid an egg* (something she did to an object).

6. *like, as*

    a. Simple explanation: Use *like* when comparing two nouns; use *as* or *as if* when comparing a noun to an idea (subject + verb).

    Not *She arranged her flowerbed as a whale* but *like a whale*.

    Not *It looks like it will be a lengthy convalescence* but *It looks as if it will be a lengthy convalescence*.

    b. When *as* means in the role, status or function of, it is a preposition.

    Treat everything here as your own.

    "Come to the Green Chapel or be known as a coward."

> The word *like* is a preposition, not a conjunction, so it starts a prepositional phrase, which ends in a noun and does not have a verb. It should not start a clause.
>
> To compare a noun to a clause, use *as, as if,* or *as though* instead of *like.*

7. *farther/farthest, further/furthest*

    Use *farther* and *farthest* as the comparative and superlative forms of *far*, referring to physical distance, no matter how short or long. Use *further* and *furthest* for everything else. *Further* means *to a greater extent* or *additional/in addition*.

    It is easy to remember the difference because *farther* and *farthest* derive from *far*, relating to distance. We do not say, "I am going fur down the road"!

    She had earned a reputation for beauty reaching into the farthest kingdoms. (physical distance)

    She swam out farther from the shore. (physical distance)

    "I will no further descant on such matters." (to a greater extent)

    Some dictionaries no longer distinguish these two, but most careful writers will.

8. *use to, used to*

    Use to is substandard English. The correct form is *used to*.

    She used to bring pictures she had drawn to Lady Constance.

9. *try and, try to*

    Use *try to* when trying to do something. *She tried to sprint across the hill* means she attempted to accomplish this feat. *She tried and sprinted across the hill* does not make sense because *tried* needs an object, as in *she tried climbing*.

10. *affect, effect*

> **a.** *Affect* as a verb means *to influence, act on,* or *produce a change in. Effect* as a noun is the result of that change. Most of the times this is how we use these words.
>
> *Years of indulgence had the obvious effect* (noun meaning the result) *of spoiling Dorinda.*
>
> *Maybe Dorinda was too self-centered for anyone else to affect* (verb form meaning to influence) *her deeply.*
>
> **b.** *Affect* and *effect* both have a noun and verb meaning, which is one reason they are so confusing. As a noun, a person's affect is his emotional appearance, feeling or emotion. As a verb, *to effect* is to bring about or accomplish something.

11. *between, among*

> Use *between* when dealing with two items, *among* with three or more.
>
> *She wandered among the exotic botanical species.* (more than two different species of plants)
>
> *Dorinda held the napkin between her thumb and first finger.* (two fingers)

Idioms

An idiom is an expression that cannot be understood literally, word for word. Example: *We had better go our separate ways. Had better* is an idiom meaning *ought to.* No one *has,* or possesses, something called *better!*

Do not expect students to determine parts of speech of words in idioms because often this will not make sense. When sentences begin with idioms, they do not always have to be labeled as certain openers.

Passive versus Active Voice (Advanced)

In active voice, the subject of the sentence is doing the verb action. Most sentences are written in active voice. Example: *The soldier invited the dwarf to warm himself by the fire.*

In passive voice, we start with the person or thing being acted upon, in the example above, the dwarf, and make it the new subject of the sentence: ***The dwarf was invited by the soldier*** *to warm himself by the fire.*

Passive voice follows this pattern: **Person/thing being acted on +** *be* **verb + past participle +** *by* **someone or something** (either in the sentence or understood). *The dwarf* (person being acted on) *was* (*be* verb) *invited* (past participle) *by the soldier* (*by* someone) *to warm himself by the fire.* If the sentence does not have all four elements, it is not in passive voice. That is, not every *be* verb is passive.

In writing, discourage older students from misusing passive voice because it is usually wordy and dull. Do not teach the concept to younger students.

Understanding passive voice helps instructors and older students even at this level with one tricky part of speech identification. When -ed past participles (see Parts of Speech: Verbals, page G-9) follow a *be* verb, it is unclear whether they are subject complements after a linking verb or part of the verb phrase.

One way to tell is that they are verbs if the sentence is in passive voice.

> Example: *The castle would be **demolished** by the soldiers.* Test for passive voice: *The castle* (subject being acted upon) *would be* (*be* verb) *demolished* (past participle) *by the*

soldiers (*by* someone). Since this sentence is in passive voice, *demolished* is a verb, not an adjective.

The men were famished. Test: *The men* (subject) *were* (be verb) *famished*. *Famished* ends in -ed, so can it be a past participle? No: there is no one *famishing* the men so no *by* someone phrase. This makes *famished* an adjective, not a verb.

Two hundred pounds would be rewarded to the man who delivered Robin Hood to the king. Test: *Two hundred pounds* (subject being acted upon) *would be* (be verb) *rewarded* (past participle) *to the man who delivered Robin Hood to the king.* There is also a "*by* someone" phrase that is understood: *by the king.* Since this is in passive voice, the past participle is part of the verb and not an adjective.

Past Perfect Tense (Advanced)

Use the past perfect when relating the earlier of two events that occurred in the past. The more recent event is couched in past tense, the earlier event in past perfect. Form past perfect with *had* + the past participle of the verb.

One such frightful deluge swept away (past tense) *worthy King William, who had reigned* (past perfect) *in Flovenia for fourteen peaceful years.*

Subjunctive Mood (Advanced)

Used infrequently, the subjunctive mood expresses contrary-to-fact conditions with wish or if statements in the third person followed by a *be* verb. For present tense, all subjects take *be*; for past, *were*. To test: Ask if the statement is literally true. If not, use subjunctive.

*Kissing his hand, the little mermaid felt as if her heart **were** already broken.* Her heart is *not* already broken, so the subjunctive is correct: "as if her heart were" rather than "as if her heart was."

*Fearing lest his name **be** tarnished, Gawain began to despair of ever finding his implacable enemy.* His name will not be tarnished, so the subjunctive is correct: not "Fearing lest his name *is* tarnished," but "Fearing lest it *be* tarnished."

Stylistic Techniques

Fix It! stories teach the stylistic techniques of the Institute for Excellence in Writing. The list below reviews these techniques and offers pointers about how dress-ups and sentence openers reinforce grammar.

Dress-Ups

Dress-ups are ways of dressing up writing style, either by using stronger vocabulary (-ly adverb; strong verb; quality adjective) or by making the sentence structure more complex (*who-which* clause; www.asia.b clause).

Generally, hold older students to a more rigorous standard than younger students, encouraging all students to use word lists like a thesaurus to build their vocabulary when they work on dress-ups in their own writing.

The words marked as vocabulary dress-ups in the book have varying levels of strength. It is up to teachers to decide whether to count some of these words as "dress-up quality" or to allow words the book does not mark. The goal is to encourage interesting and specific vocabulary.

Two of the dress-ups, -ly adverbs and www.asia.b clauses, can also be sentence openers if they start a sentence. Count them as dress-ups if they come later in the sentence but as sentence openers if they are the first word in the sentence.

-ly Adverbs

Found anywhere except the first word in a sentence, this dress-up enriches by adding color and detail. Like other adverbs, the -ly adverb describes or modifies adjectives or verbs. See Parts of Speech: Adverbs, page G-10.

> The palace accountant *vehemently* complained about the princess's excessive texting.

Count only -ly words that are adverbs, not imposter -ly's, which are adjectives, like *princely, lonely, ugly,* and *ghastly*.

When they are ready, direct students to distinguish true -ly adverbs from adjectives by understanding how these parts of speech work. Even younger students can be asked what part of speech follows the -ly word.

The easiest way to check if an -ly word is an adverb or adjective is to place it in front of a noun. If that makes sense, it must be an imposter -ly (an adjective) since only adjectives can describe nouns. Then check it by placing it in front of a verb. If it works, it is a legitimate -ly adverb.

Examples: *She **cleverly** masqueraded herself as a poor girl.* *Cleverly* comes before and describes a verb (*masqueraded*), so it must be an -ly adverb. It also answers the adverb question *how: She masqueraded. How did she masquerade? She cleverly masqueraded.*

*"What nonsense this **silly** frog is talking!"* *Silly* comes before and describes a noun (*frog*), so it must be an imposter -ly, an adjective and not an adverb. It also does not answer the adverb question *how.*

Who-Which Clauses

A *who-which* clause is a dependent clause that begins with *who* or *which*. These clauses deepen content by adding new information to the sentence or minimize choppiness by combining two short sentences. See also Sentences, Clauses, and Phrases: Clauses, page G-16.

Example: *Robin Hood cut straight a hefty staff, **which** measured six feet in length.*

To keep the *who* or *which* from stealing the main verb, remove the *who-which* clause from the sentence and confirm that a complete thought (a sentence) remains. If not, the *who* or *which* may have stolen the main verb.

Example: *A bedraggled young woman, **who** stood at the door.* If I remove my who clause, I am left with only *A bedraggled young woman*, which is not a complete thought. I need something more: *A bedraggled young woman, who stood at the door, dripped water into her shoes.*

Use *who* for people, *which* for things or institutions. Animals are a special category. If they are just animals, use *which*. If they are beloved pets or if they take on human characteristics like the frog in "The Frog Prince," use *who*.

Younger students should form *who-which* clauses by placing the *who* or *which* immediately after the noun it describes. Many *who-which* clauses take commas. For younger students, you could simply require that they put commas around them all and only later teach essential and nonessential *who-which* clauses.

Advanced *Who-Which* Clauses

Punctuation. *Who-which* clauses are set off with commas if they are **nonessential** but take no commas if they are **essential.**

Essential which clauses usually start with *that* instead of *which*, but do not count these as dress-ups because the dress-up is for practicing who and which clauses.

That starts an adjective clause when it follows a noun. If it follows a verb, it is a noun clause instead. See under Punctuation: Commas: Rule 15: Essential-Nonessential Elements, page G-24, for further information about this important concept. See also Stylistic Techniques: Advanced Style: Noun Clauses, page G-44.

Question. When *who* or *which* asks a question, it begins a full sentence (a main clause), so *who* or *which* starting a question is not a *who-which* adjective clause, which is a dependent clause. Example: "Who was at the door?" does not count as a dress-up.

Whose. *Whose* is the possessive pronoun, used with people or things.

Examples: There lived within the glades of Sherwood Forest a famous outlaw *whose* name was Robin Hood. The table *whose* legs were wobbly threatened to crash to the ground.

Who versus whom. Use *whom* instead of *who* when *whom* is the object of something (objective case), such as the object of a preposition or a direct object. Use *who* when it is

Who-which clauses are adjective clauses, which usually modify the noun they follow. Older students may write which clauses to modify the entire idea that comes before.

Example: You have killed the king's deer, which is a capital offense. It is not the deer that is the offense but killing it— the full idea expressed in the main clause.

Advanced: The pronouns *who, that,* and *which* become singular or plural according to the noun they modify. Since the clause modifies the noun right before it, the verb must agree in number with that noun.

Example: Gawain was one of the knights who honor courtesy. The verb honor agrees with knights, not with one.

Also, if you teach *who-which* clauses as a dependent clause, it may help to understand that who or which is usually the subject of the clause.

in the subjective case, functioning as the subject of the sentence or, rarely, as a subject complement. See Parts of Speech: Pronouns, page G-7.

Trick: *he/him* substitution. If you can revise the sentence and substitute *he* or *they*, use *who*; if *him* or *them*, use *whom*.

> *He bellowed his challenge, as if doubting* **who/whom** *in the hall held rule. He* held rule, so *who* is correct.

> *I am not he of* **who/whom** *you speak.* You speak of *him*, so *whom*. (object of preposition)

Invisible *who-which*. Who-which's followed by a *be* verb can be invisible for a more stylish sentence.

> Example: *Robin Hood started off from Locksley, ~~which was~~ the town where he lived. All had come to Sherwood Forest, ~~which was~~ a vast, uncharted wood.* In both cases, we could drop *which was* for a more elegant construction.

Strong Verbs

Teach younger students to recognize verbs by filling in these blanks with a form of the word in question: *yesterday he _____; today he _____; tomorrow he will _____.* (Yesterday he pitched; today he pitches; tomorrow he will pitch.)

As the most powerful part of speech, the verb can make or break a sentence. Challenge students to distinguish truly strong verbs from ordinary ones.

> Example: Compare ordinary: "It'll be the first thing I'll throw away when I make changes."

> versus strong: "It'll be the first thing I'll pitch when I redecorate."

Strong verb dress-ups should be action verbs, not helping or linking verbs. See Parts of Speech: Verbs, page G-8.

Quality Adjectives

Gradually teach students the difference between ordinary and quality adjectives. Quality adjectives are strong because they are more colorful, provide a stronger image or feeling, or add more detail and are more specific than ordinary adjectives. See also Parts of Speech: Adjectives, page G-10.

> Example: His advisers realized they had a *daunting* task.

Adjectives describe nouns. Teach how to locate adjectives with this simple test: The _____ person or object (thing).

> Examples: *the gurgling brook.* Is *brook* a person or thing? Yes, so *gurgling* is an adjective. Or *the confident stranger.* Is *stranger* a person or object? Yes, so *confident*, which describes the noun, must be an adjective.

www.asia.b Clauses

Initially, teach that dependent clauses may begin with one of these eight subordinating conjunctions: *when, while, where, as, since, if, although, because,* easy to learn by memorizing **www.asia.b**. IEW materials sometimes call these **the www words**. They usually start an adverb clause.

Eventually, students will learn that other words can start dependent clauses too, such as *until, whereas, wherever, whenever, as if, unless,* and sometimes *before* or *after*. See Sentences, Clauses, and Phrases: Clauses, page G-16, and Stylistic Techniques: Sentence Openers: #5 Clausal, page G-42.

A dependent clause cannot stand on its own as a sentence. It needs to be attached to a main clause to be a legal sentence.

Examples:

"Meet me *if* you dare."

"Your name, Little John, fits you ill *because* you are far from little!"

Robin Hood and his band guffawed loudly *until* the stranger began to grow enraged.

Remain on the other side *while* I quickly make a staff.

Most of the time, a www.asia.b word will begin an adverb clause. When an adverb clause occurs mid-sentence (the dress-up), it should not be set off with commas; when an adverb clause starts a sentence (the opener), it takes a comma after the clause. Teach simple patterns to help students remember these rules:

MC AC: no comma when an adverb clause falls in the middle or at the end of a sentence

AC, MC: comma at the end of a clause when the adverb clause comes before the main clause

Advanced: www.asia.b Words

The www words **since**, **as**, and **until** sometimes are prepositions instead of conjunctions. You can tell they do not start clauses if there is no subject and verb after them, as in *since childhood* or *as an archer* or *until the next day*. See under Sentence Openers: #5 Clausal Opener, page G-42, for tricks to tell the difference.

The www words **as**, **where**, and **when** can start adjective clauses instead of adverb clauses, usually when they follow and describe a noun. Adjective clauses can be essential (no commas) or nonessential (commas). See Punctuation: Commas: Rule 15: Essential-Nonessential Elements, page G-24.

Example: *King Arthur decided to climb to the top of the cliff, where he could drink from the pool of water collected above.* This *where* clause follows a noun that it also describes; since it is nonessential, it needs a comma.

While, **although**, and **whereas** sometimes need a comma before them because they present a contrast to the main clause in the sentence.

Examples: You stand there with a lethal bow to shoot at my heart, *while* I have only a plain blackthorn staff to meet you with.

Hrothgar and Robert had been trying to save his life all along, *whereas* he had been too foolish to listen to them.

While and *whereas* technically function as coordinating conjunctions in this case and follow the punctuation pattern **MC, cc MC**, but it is easiest to explain this as needing a comma because of the contrast.

Sentence Openers

Sentence openers are the patterns that sentences begin with. Their obvious advantage is in encouraging more complex sentence structure and variety, which greatly improves the quality of student writing. A second advantage is that openers teach lots of grammar in a backdoor fashion. By teaching the patterns and punctuation that accompany the openers, you will help students master quite a bit of grammar in the context of writing.

#1 Subject Opener

Subject openers essentially begin with the subject of a main clause, although articles and/ or adjectives may precede it. If the sentence is shorter than six words, it can be counted as a #6 vss opener instead.

> Examples: *He became livid on the subject of modern gadgets.* The subject is *He.*

> *The convivial company congregated in the great hall.* The subject is *company*, but it is still a subject opener because *the* is an article and *convivial* an adjective.

Sometimes #1 sentences invert the usual word order, placing the verb or other word first. For this reason, it helps to explain that the #1 sentence starts with a main clause.

> Example: *There were blameless, loyal men at his side who rambled with him through the greenwood shades.* The actual subject is *men*, but the sentence begins with a main clause so is still a #1 subject opener.

#2 Prepositional Opener

Prepositions begin phrases that follow this pattern:

preposition + noun (no verb)

The phrase starts with a preposition and ends with a noun, with no verb inside. Other words may squeeze in between the preposition and noun but never a verb. See under #5 Clausal Opener, page G-42, for the trick to distinguish between #2s and #5s. See also Parts of Speech: Prepositions, page G-11.

Examples:

> *During* these reflections, King Morton shook his head in abject despair.

> *After* a pause she summed it up.

Younger students should practice finding prepositional phrases before identifying the #2 opener, showing how the phrase fits the pattern. Example: After (preposition) + a (article) + pause (noun). This phrase begins with a preposition, ends with a noun, and has no verb, which fits the pattern. Remind students that the lack of a verb means it must be a phrase and cannot be a clause.

Punctuation: Prepositional phrases of five or more words take a comma after them; with fewer than five, the comma is optional. Let the pause test be your guide for shorter prepositional phrases: use a comma if you need a pause, no comma if you do not.

When short prepositional openers work transitionally (as in *For example, In addition, On the other hand*), they will need a comma, just as any transitional opener should take a comma. Usually the pause test is sufficient to determine this.

Punctuation rule note: Grammar books express the punctuation rule more vaguely: long prepositional phrases take a comma; with short ones, the comma is optional.

For most students, a clear cutoff is more helpful than this general principle, and five or more words are usually long enough to warrant a comma.

Advanced Prepositional Phrase

Disguised #2. Sentences starting with some kind of time (*Wednesday; Two weeks ago; The evening of the ball; One night*) followed by the main clause begin with what is effectively a disguised #2, in which a preposition is implied but not stated, as in "One morning..." where "In," "On," or "During one morning" is implied. The sentence sounds better without the preposition, but the opener functions as if it were there and is punctuated the same way.

Infinitives. Although infinitives do not fit the usual pattern of prepositional phrases (**preposition + noun**), the *to* in them is still a preposition, used to mark the infinitive of a verb. Infinitives starting sentences may be counted as #2 openers. E.g., *To lend* credence to this claim, one of the most respected authors related a pertinent account.

#3 -ly Adverb Opener

The main difference between an -ly dress-up and -ly sentence opener is the flow of the sentence. Beginning the sentence with the -ly adverb gives a different kind of rhythm than placing it later in the sentence. Usually -ly openers do not need a comma, but let the pause test be your guide: use a comma if you want a pause, no comma if you do not.

> Examples: *Resentfully* the stranger answered him.

> *Sadly*, his amiable wife, Queen Mary, was traveling with him at the time.

Advanced: -ly Adverb Punctuation. If the -ly adverb opener modifies just the main verb, the comma is optional but discouraged. Add it only if a strong pause is desired.

> *Resentfully the stranger answered him. The stranger resentfully answered him* also makes sense, so *resentfully* modifies just the verb and a comma is therefore not needed.

If the -ly adverb opener modifies the entire sentence, the comma is required.

> *Sadly, his wife was traveling with him at the time of the massive flood. Sadly* describes the whole sentence, so a comma after it is needed.

Tip to distinguish: The -ly adverb modifies the sentence and takes a comma if you can convert it into the phrase "it is _____ that" with the adjective form of that adverb in the blank.

> *It is sad that his wife was traveling with him at the time.* We can convert *sadly* into "it is sad that," so this -ly adverb modifies the sentence and takes a comma.

> *It is resentful that the stranger answered him.* Here, the -ly adverb *resentfully* does not make sense as "it is resentful that," so it fails the sentence modifying test and therefore does not need a comma.

Sometimes, both the comma and no comma are correct but affect the meaning.

> *Sorrowfully Chanticleer acceded to the counsel of his wife.* He acceded, but he did so sorrowfully, with regret.

> *Sorrowfully, Chanticleer acceded to the counsel of his wife.* This opener is the narrator's warning that Chanticleer made a mistake in acceding to his wife's advice. It is sorrowful that Chanticleer acceded to his wife's counsel.

#4 -ing Participial Phrase Opener

Sentence opener #4 sounds easy but can be complicated grammatically. Teach this pattern:

-ing word/phrase + comma + subject/-inger + main verb

It begins with an -ing word (participle) or phrase, then a comma, then the subject of the main clause which is also doing the inging, then the main verb. Check that #4 openers have these four elements and teach students to ask this important question: Is the subject after the comma doing the inging?

Examples: *Gathering their three gifts, the soldiers set out on a journey to visit a neighboring king.* 1. *Gathering their three gifts* is an -ing phrase; 2. there is a comma; 3. the noun after the comma is both the subject of the main clause (*soldiers set out*) and the inger (*soldiers were gathering*); 4. *set out* is the verb. This follows the four steps and is therefore a legal, legitimate #4 opener.

Taking up his bow, Robin Hood shot with unparalleled skill. This also follows the four steps: Robin is both taking up his bow and shooting.

Advanced #4 Opener

There are two main ways students might mislabel #4s.

1. Illegal #4s look like #4s, only the person or thing after the comma is not the one doing the inging. This is known as a **dangling modifier**—an often humorous but still grammatically faulty sentence pattern.

Examples: *Hopping quickly to keep up, she let the frog traipse behind her to the resplendent dining hall.* It is not the princess but the frog that is supposed to be hopping!

Looming nearby in the harbor, she beheld a large ship. The mermaid is not looming nearby but the ship.

Scanning the noble assembly, the horse rode straight to the high dais. The horse is not the one doing the scanning but the Green Knight.

2. Imposter #4s begin with an -ing word so look like #4s but are actually #1 subject openers or #2 prepositional phrase openers. See also Parts of Speech: Verbals, page G-9.

#2s that look like #4s begin with one of these prepositions: *during, according to, regarding, concerning.* The four steps reveal that the pattern does not work.

Examples: *According to state history, the only indisputable test for real princess blood is the mattress test.* The subject after the comma is *test*, which is not doing the *according*, so this sentence does not fit the #4 pattern. It is actually a #2.

During the obligatory dance after dinner, she twirled him around. She is not doing the inging. In fact, nobody can "dure" because *during* is not a participle derived from a verb but a preposition.

#1s that look like #4s begin with an -ing word, but it functions as the subject of the sentence. (We call -ing nouns gerunds, not participles). These have no place for a comma and no person or thing mentioned doing the inging.

Examples: *Living at the splendid castle cheered the soldiers.* There is no comma or place for one, nor is there a subject that is doing the inging. The context makes it clear that the soldiers are living there, but the sentence does not use *soldiers* as the subject doing that action. The subject-verb pair is *Living cheered.*

Peering through the curtain left Gawain in wonder. Again, no comma or place for one. The subject-verb pair is *Peering left.*

Invisible #4s are sentences that follow the same pattern as regular #4s, but the -ing word is hidden. These sentences begin with an adjective or adjective phrase followed by a comma plus main clause, with the word *being, seeming,* or *appearing* implied at the beginning of the sentence. They are more elegant without the -ing participle but function and are punctuated just like a #4.

IEW instructors sometimes add a seventh opener for sentences starting with a past participle ending in -ed, but it is unnecessary to create a separate category for this since it follows the same pattern as an invisible -ing opener.

Examples: *Quick-witted and agile, Robert compensated for his limitation by an eagerness to please.* Implied: *Appearing quick-witted and agile, Robert compensated for his limitation.*

Relaxed and untroubled, the stranger genially waited for him. Implied: *Being relaxed and untroubled, the stranger genially waited for him.*

Energized by boyish blood, Arthur did not care to lounge at his ease. Implied: *Being energized by boyish blood, Arthur did not care to lounge at his ease.*

#5 Clausal Opener

This is the same as the dress-up and uses the same www words (subordinating conjunctions), except that now this dependent clause starts the sentence and needs a comma after it. Teach the simple pattern: **AC, MC**

Examples:

If possessions were plundered, the yeomen would recapture the goods and return them to the poor.

As he approached, Robin Hood noticed a tall stranger resolutely striding toward the bridge.

When he demanded it back, Dorinda mumbled something about not being able to locate it.

Advanced: #5s versus #2s. The problem with accurately identifying #5s, #2s, and www.asia.b dress-ups is that a few words might be either a preposition or a subordinating conjunction. *After, before, since, until* and *as* can function as either, and while *because* is a subordinating conjunction, *because of* is a preposition.

Two tricks help tell the difference, both bouncing off the fact that prepositional phrases never have a verb and clauses always do.

1. Drop the first word of the phrase or clause in question and look at what is left. If it is a sentence, the group of words is an adverb clause; if it is not, the words form a prepositional phrase.

2. Look for a verb: only #5s and adverb clause dress-ups can have a verb.

Example:

a. After supper, King Morton ordered Dorinda to prepare the Golden Guestroom.

b. After they finished supper, King Morton ordered Dorinda to prepare the Golden Guestroom.

Drop *After* and see what is left in the opener. Sentence *a* starts with a #2 prepositional opener because *supper* is not a complete sentence; sentence *b* starts with a #5 clausal opener because *they finished supper* is a complete sentence. Also, we know that sentence *b* starts with a #5 because the opener contains a verb (*finished*).

#6 vss, or Very Short Sentence

An occasional short sentence can pack a punch in paragraphs that otherwise have intricate and lengthy sentences.

Examples:

"Tarry for me here."

Robin Hood set off.

The blow inflamed him.

King Morton esteemed values.

The trick to #6s is that they must be short (two to five words) and they must be sentences (subject + verb and be able to stand alone).

They should also be strong: a vsss = Very Short Strong Sentence!

#T or Transitional Opener

#T works for sentences beginning with interjections, interrupters, or transitional words and expressions. Transitional openers are usually followed by a comma.

Common words and phrases in this class include the following: *however, therefore, then, thus, later, now, otherwise, indeed, first, next, also, moreover, hence, furthermore, henceforth, likewise*. Also included are interjections, such as *oh, ouch, wow, ha*, which can be followed by a comma or an exclamation mark.

Tip: When you add one of these words or phrases to a main clause, the clause remains a main clause.

#T "Moreover, the august Macrobius explained that his dreams were clear portents." (transition)

#T Oh, how gladly she would have shaken off all this pomp and laid aside the heavy wreath! (interjection)

#T "Alas! For this, you have forfeited my heart and all my love." (exclamatory interjection)

#Q or Question

#Q takes care of sentences that ask questions. This teaches students not to mark questions beginning with *who* or *which* as their *who-which* dress-up or questions beginning with words like *when* or *where* as their clausal openers.

#Q Did you ever hear the story of the three poor soldiers?

#Q "What name do you go by, good fellow?"

#Q Where is fair Pertelote?

Advanced Style

Duals and Triples

Deliberate use of dual or triple adverbs, adjectives, or verbs, especially when the words add a different nuance, enriches prose and challenges students to be precise with words chosen. Classic writers of the past like Charles Dickens and persuasive essayists like Winston Churchill have used duals and triples to convey their meaning most powerfully.

Examples:

All who beheld her wondered at her *graceful, swaying* movements.

The ship glided away *smoothly and lightly* over the tranquil sea.

Noun Clauses

A noun clause is a dependent clause used as a noun. It can function in any of the ways that nouns function: subject, direct or indirect object, or object of a preposition. See also Sentences, Clauses, and Phrases: Clauses: Dependent Clauses (Advanced): Noun Clauses, page G-18.

Although noun clauses may begin with many words, those starting with *that* are the main ones highlighted in IEW because students sometimes confuse them with essential adjective clauses.

To tell the difference: If *that* begins an adjective clause, you can substitute *which* and it will still make sense. If *that* begins a noun clause, *which* does not work in its place. Also, noun clauses follow verbs and answer the question "What?" after a verb. Adjective clauses usually follow a noun and describe the noun they come immediately after.

Example:

"I know well that I am the weakest of these illustrious knights." Can you say, "I know well which I am the weakest of knights"? No, so it is not an adjective clause but a noun clause. It follows a verb (*know*) and answers the question "What?" E.g., *I know.* What does he know? That he is the weakest of these knights.

Invisible Noun Clause: This is a noun clause with the word *that* understood, not stated directly. Example: *He could tell [that] he was going to relish his palace stay.* Sometimes it is more elegant without *that*: *He could tell he was going to relish his palace stay.*

Decorations

Used sparingly, as an artist might add a splash of bright color to a nature painting, these stylistic techniques daringly or delicately decorate one's prose. You can introduce the decorations at any time when teaching IEW writing.

The six decorations are questions, conversation/quotation, 3sss (three short staccato sentences), dramatic opening-closing, simile/metaphor, and alliteration. In *Fix It! Grammar*, you will see the last two.

Similes and Metaphors

A simile is a comparison between two unlike things using the words *like* or *as*. A metaphor, harder to create, is a similar comparison but without the *like* or *as*.

Examples:

The ship dived like a swan between them. (simile)

The waves rose mountains high. (metaphor)

The key to recognizing these figures of speech is that they compare unlike things. For example, to say that a cat is like a tiger is a comparison but not a simile.

Alliteration

Alliteration is the repetition of the same initial consonant sounds in two or more words in close proximity. It adds flavor to writing when used judiciously.

Example: *Arthur was **seeking some** shady relief from the **sweltering sun**. Shady* is not part of the alliteration because it does not have the same initial sound as the other *s* words. It is not the letter that matters but the sound. Thus, *celery* and *sound* are alliterative, but *shady* and *sound* are not.

Stressed syllables in the middle of words that carry the same sound can contribute to the alliteration. Example: *I **will award** you **what** I **win** in the **woods**.*

In academic writing, alliteration usually sounds awkward unless found in a title or the first or last sentence of a paper, where it can appropriately dramatize those parts.